IF IT WASN'T FOR CELIBACY...

I WOULD HAVE BEEN A PRIEST

I0160397

Reality Checks on Religion, Politics and Life

By **Frank Hegyi**

Some of the stories were published in
Frank Hegyi's Corner

CanAsian Times
A National Weekly Newspaper

Support by

cistel

Cistel Technology Inc.
is gratefully acknowledged.

Published by
Frank Hegyi Publications
www.hegyipublicationa.com

© Frank Hegyi - 2009

ISBN 978-0-9812495-3-7

Table of Contents

ABOUT RELIGION

If it wasn't for celibacy I would be a priest

The day after I was born, my mother got out of her bed and took me to the church to be baptised. She was told by the Roman Catholic parish priest that if I died before baptism, my soul would linger in purgatory and I would not be admitted to heaven. My mother followed the teachings of the church to the letter. When I was in grade school, I did well in catechism studies and the parish priest informed my mother that I had the qualities to study to be a priest. My mother was ecstatic. It was the wish of every mother in the village that one of her sons becomes a priest.

When I finished grade 8, my mother enrolled me in a seminary, secretly still wishing that I may become a priest, although she reassured me that it was for the purpose of getting a high school education in a religious environment. But, to the disappointment of my mother, the seminary was shut down by the communist regime before I was admitted. I wasn't unhappy about that because by that time I was getting to like girls more than being an altar boy.

Mandatory celibacy was an unquestionable condition for priesthood in the 1950's. The reason given for this requirement was that the cleric be closer to God in the fulfillment of his duties. At the time I was confused about this because our parish priest had a son with the house keeper and one of our assistant priests eloped with the lead singer of the choir who was expecting his child. The gossip that developed in our village around these two irregularities was labelled by my father as "preaching water but drinking wine" (father used this expression quite liberally each time he disagreed with the ultra conservative religious leaders).

Over the years my views became rather liberal concerning Christian denominations. I got married in a Presbyterian church, I also taught Sunday School there, and through involvement in service club (Kiwanis) activities I had interactions with other denominations. I found good in all of these denominations while at the same time observed the personal influences, both positive and negative, of the various religious leaders.

Prior to her death in the early 1990's my mother urged me to return to "our" church for worship. Out of respect for her, my wife (also a former Roman Catholic) and I now attend masses regularly in "our' church. In the light of the increasing shortages of priests and the recent public apologies by Pope Benedict XVI about sexual abuses of Catholic clergy, I started to reflect on my past concerns about the denomination my mother was unquestionably faithful to throughout her life.

In my opinion, the root of the problem appears to be the mandatory requirement of celibacy. If it wasn't for that, the structure of leadership would be more balanced and would include married men and women (yes Women!!) who could be good role models for the youth of the church. Celibacy is a man-made rule of the church, became a requirement mainly during the reign of Pope Gregory VII (1073-1085). Prior to that, priests, bishops and even popes were married. The rational used by Pope Gregory was based on the fact that Kings and nobles donated property to the Roman Catholic Church in exchange for the faithful service of priests. Some priests tried to leave this property to their heirs. In addition, they had loyalty to the nobles who provided them with homes. Pope Gregory wanted to protect Church property, and to ensure that the loyalty of the priests went to the Pope and not to secular rulers.

Since returning to my mother's church, I have introduced our two youngest grandchildren to the catholic faith. When Sara was baptized, I was day dreaming that she will have a wonderful future in Canada, can achieve anything she decides to go after, except becoming a priest because she is a girl. I thought only my grandson will be able to go in that direction if he chooses. But then, a few days ago Ryan came home from school (he is in grade I) and announced with a big smile: "Papa, I got a girlfriend". Well, I guess neither of them will be clerics unless they join another denomination!

Religious pilgrimages good for the soul

On September 15, 2008, Pope Benedict XVI visited Lourdes in France, the shrine where a 14-year old peasant girl, Bernadette Soubirous, claimed that she had seen a "lady" on February 11, 1858 in the cave. Initially nobody believed her and she was even prohibited by her parents to visit the place again. But, under the protection of darkness at night time, she went there again on March 25, when she was told by the "lady": "I am the Immaculate Conception". The shrine at Lourdes is now one of the most important pilgrimage places for Christians; 4-6 million visit there annually and the head of the Roman Catholic church celebrated this September with thousands of believers the 150th anniversary of the apparitions of Our Lady of Lourdes.

Pilgrimage is a journey or search of great moral significance. Sometimes, it is a journey to a sacred place or shrine of importance to a person's beliefs. Members of many major religions participate in pilgrimages. For example, Buddhism offers four sites of pilgrimage: the Buddha's birthplace at Kapilavastu, the site where he attained Enlightenment Bodh Gaya, where he first preached at Benares, and where he achieved Parinirvana at Kusinagara. In Islamic religion, Hajj is a pilgrimage to Mecca, it is the largest annual pilgrimage in the world. It is the fifth pillar of Islam, an obligation that must be carried out at least once in their lifetime by every able-bodied Muslim who can afford to do so. It is a demonstration of the solidarity of the Muslim people, and their submission to Allah. The Holy Land acts as a focal point for the pilgrimages of many religions, such as Judaism, Christianity, Islam and the Bahá'í Faith. In addition, there are many lesser known pilgrimage sites where miracles claimed to have been witnessed.

When I was growing up in Central Europe and served regularly as altar boy in the Roman Catholic Church, I participated in annual pilgrimages where village people walked in procession for 20 km to the Holly Well Chapel of the Queen of Rosary in Vasvar. The valley of Holy Well (Szentkút) is a famous place of pilgrimage in Hungary. The simple Classical chapel was built at the Well in 1863. The story goes that a hussar soldier regained his sight after washing his eyes in the spring water. He built the chapel to show his gratitude to God and the Virgin Mary.

Our processions to the Holly Well Chapel usually consisted of about 200 people, 5 by 40 persons in an orderly column, with the priest and 2 altar boys in the middle. The priest and about 5 parishioners would chant one-liner prayers after which all would respond "Maria help us" or "Lord hear our prayer". Most people participated in this pilgrimage to be closer to God, asking for God's blessing, asking for God's forgiveness, and the sick came (usually on a horse drawn carriage following the procession) hoping for a miracle cure. When after the 1956 revolution I ended up in refugee camps, my mother continued this pilgrimage, praying to the Virgin Mary to protect me in foreign lands. Every year I got a new picture from her of the Holy Well Chapel, blessed by our parish priest or the Bishop, and she asked me to carry it with me for protection. I believe that the pilgrimage helped during my lifetime, at least the picture was a symbol of my mother's love, I wasn't alone especially in those early years when I struggled to re-build a shattered life. At the same time it helped my mother, she was comforted in her belief that she was still able to protect her son. Now that I am a grandfather, I appreciate the importance of this a lot more than I did at the time it was occurring.

I believe that religious pilgrimages helps millions of people around the world in attaining inner peace with their creator and getting comforted when facing difficulties in everyday life.

Religion or Tradition

The Supreme Court of Canada ruled 4-3 on Friday, July 24th 2009 that the Hutterian Brethren of Wilson Colony, located east of Lethbridge, Alberta must abide by provincial rules that make a digital photo mandatory for all new driver's licenses. Members of the colony believe that the Bible's second commandment: "Thou shalt not make unto thee any graven image" — prohibits them from having their photograph willingly taken.

Originating in the Austrian province of Tyrol in the 16th century, the forerunners of the Hutterites migrated to Moravia (now part of Czech Republic) to escape persecution. There, under the leadership of Jakob Hutter, they developed the communal form of living based on the New Testament books of the Acts of the Apostles (Chapters 2, 4, and 5) and 2 Corinthians. A basic ideology of Hutterian society has always been absolute pacifism, forbidding its members from taking part in military activities, taking orders, wearing a formal uniform or contributing to war taxes. This has led to expulsion or persecution in the several lands in which they have lived. In Moravia, the Hutterites flourished for over a century, until renewed persecution caused by the Austrian takeover

17

of the Czech lands forced them once again to migrate, first to Transylvania (Hungary) and then, in the early 18th century, to Ukraine (Russian Empire). After sending scouts to North America in 1873 along with a Mennonite delegation, three groups totaling 1,265 individuals migrated to North America between 1874 and 1879 in order to escape from the new Russian military service law. Most of the groups settled in Dakota Territory and central Montana where they established the traditional Hutterite communal lifestyle. Following that, several state laws were enacted seeking to deny Hutterites religious legal status to their communal farms (colonies). However, by this time some Hutterites moved and established new colonies in Alberta and Saskatchewan. During World War I, the pacifist Hutterites suffered persecution in the United States. The Hutterite community responded by abandoning Dakota and moving 17 of the 18 existing American colonies to the Canadian provinces of Alberta, Manitoba, and Saskatchewan. Today, approximately three of every four Hutterite colonies are in Canada with almost all of the remainder in the United States (primarily South Dakota and Montana). The total Hutterite population in both countries is estimated around 50,000.

Hutterite communes depend largely on farming or ranching for their income. Some colonies are getting into manufacturing as it gets harder to make a living on farming alone. Colonies are virtually self-sufficient, constructing their own buildings, doing their own maintenance and repair on equipment and making their own clothes. Hutterite colonies are male-managed with women participating in traditional roles such as cooking, medical decisions, and selection and purchase of fabric for clothing. Each colony has three high-level leaders. The two top-level leaders are the Minister and the Secretary. A third leader is the Assistant Minister. The Minister also holds the position as President in matters related to the incorporation of the legal business entity associated with each colony. The Secretary is widely referred to as the colony "Boss" or "Business Boss" and is responsible for the business operations of the colony—book-keeping, cheque-writing, and budget organizer. The Assistant Minister helps in church leadership (preaching) responsibilities, but will often also be the Teacher for the school-age children (http://en.wikipedia.org/wiki/Hutterite)

While the ideology of Hutterites is firmly rooted in the Bible, their way of life reflects traditional developments where some practices are rigidly followed, while others have adjusted to technological developments. For example, meals are taken by the entire colony in a dining or fellowship room; men and women sit at separate tables and the men eat first. On the other hand, farming equipment technology generally matches or exceeds that of non-Hutterite farmers. Cell phones are common among groups and text messaging has made cell phones particularly useful for Hutterian young people wishing to keep in touch with their peers. Computers and internet access have penetrated many homes, especially where young people reside.

Religions should promote peace

Pope Benedict XVI said on Easter Sunday (April 12th 2009) that reconciliation was the only way to resolve the Israeli-Palestinian conflict, and that the entire world needed to rediscover hope to end wars, poverty and financial turmoil. "At a time of world food shortage, of financial turmoil, of old and new forms of poverty, of disturbing climate change, of violence and deprivation which force many to leave their homelands in search of a less precarious form of existence, of the ever present threat of terrorism, of growing fears over the future, it is urgent to rediscover grounds for hope," he said.

Religions of the World can play an important part in providing hope for the people of the world to live in harmony. In particular, religious leaders have the opportunity of providing leadership and education to the faithful by stating that killing human beings is wrong, especially when some extremists encourage such evil acts to be performed in the name of "God".

It is also important that religious leaders thrive to remove double standards when it comes to poverty. Living in luxurious accommodations and lifestyles of great abundances can be termed as preaching water while drinking wine. There is an opportunity for more religious leaders to work on the front lines among the poor and hence show leadership by example.

Religious practices (including dogma) that can be hazardous to the health and welfare of the faithful also need reconciliation. For example, the opposition of the Roman Catholic Church to the use of condoms appears to be in conflict with attempts by the World Health Organization to reduce the spread of aids.

When we look at the proportion of the world population that appears to practice a certain form of religion, the numbers clearly show the opportunities that religions leaders have in promoting hope for the world. These numbers are detailed on the following website:

http://www.adherents.com/Religions_By_Adherents.html#Christianity

Major religions ranked by number of adherents are summarized below as follows:

Christianity: 2.1 billion
Islam: 1.5 billion
Hinduism: 900 million
Chinese traditional religion: 394 million
Buddhism: 376 million
Primal indigenous: 300 million
African traditional and diasporic: 100 million
Sikhism: 23 million
Juche: 19 million
Spiritism: 15 million

Judaism: 14 million
Baha'i: 7 million
Jainism: 4.2 million
Shinto: 4 million
Cao Dai: 4 million
Zoroastrianism: 2.6 million
Tenrikvo: 2 million
Unitarian-universalism: 800,000
Rastafariansm: 600,000
Scientology: 500,000

The secular/non-religious/agnostic/atheist portion of the world's population is over 1.1 billion or 16%.

Since over 80% of the world's population is categorized (not necessarily practicing) as belonging to religious denominations, religious leaders have a major opportunity of promoting world peace, reducing poverty and helping to raise the standard of living in most parts of the world.

"There's Probably No God"

OC Transpo officials previously decided not to allow the ads, which read: "There's probably no God, now stop worrying and enjoy your life". But on March 11th Ottawa city council, after seeking legal advice, has approved a motion that will allow billboard ads to appear on the city's buses that question the existence of God.

Apparently, the campaign was triggered on June 19th 2008 when a Guardian reporter/comedy writer, Ariane Sherine was walking to work and saw ads on two buses "When the son of man comes, will he find faith on the earth?" (Luke 18:8) followed by the web address: http://www.jesussaid.org/ Ariane was particularly offended by a message on the web site which warned anyone who doesn't accept the word of Jesus: "You will be condemned to everlasting separation from God and then you spend all eternity in torment in hell. Jesus spoke about this as a lake of fire which was prepared for the devil and all his angels (demonic spirits)" (Matthew 25:41). She then called the Advertising Standards Authority to complain and was told that the quotations used are clearly from the Bible and there's nothing in the advertising standards code to prohibit advertising a religious message. Then she questioned another unrelated ad by Carlsberg that said that their lager was "probably the best lager in the world". Further investigation revealed that Carlsberg used the word "probably" to prevent jealous rivals calling in the lawyers and adds a touch of modesty to what is otherwise a simple, big, untrue – and effective – boast.

Ariane was supported in her campaign by leading secularists who jumped on board to help raise the money and after a six-week fundraising effort in which nearly 1,000 people pledged money to counter what they said was an unfair pro-religion bias in the advertising world. The initial goal was to raise £11,000 to fund two sets of atheist adverts on 30 London buses for four weeks. However, with the help of the British Humanist Association (BHA) and the prominent atheist Professor Richard Dawkins, the campaign raised £135,000 Given this unexpected amount, Ariane announced on January 6, 2009 that "800 buses – instead of the 30 we were initially aiming for – are now rolling out across the UK with the slogan, "There's probably no God. Now stop worrying and enjoy your life", in locations all over England, Scotland and Wales, including Manchester, Edinburgh, Glasgow, York, Cardiff, Devon, Leeds, Bristol and Aberdeen". This campaign has now moved to the international arena and its effectiveness seems to be linked to the word "probably" which makes people think!

The Toronto Transit Commission approved the advertisements on the commission's buses, trams, and metro and rapid transit trains. Following a request by the Association humaniste du Québec, the Société des transports de Montréal, Canada, accepted the proposed message "Dieu n'existe probablement pas, alors cessez de vous inquiéter et profitez de la vie" (a translation of the original UK advert) and the bus took the road during March 2009. Secular Humanists and Free Thinkers in Halifax and London and have had their adverts refused, while religious group have previously advertised in those cities. In British Columbia, Vancouver, Victoria and Kelowna adverts were barred on the ground that no religious advertisement is allowed on buses.

The ads are likely to offend many believers, especially some of the elderly as they are preparing for their final journey, as well as will confuse some young people about this delicate topic. For this reason it would make sense to bar all religious (especially the scare tactic ones) and atheist ads on the buses.

Tunnel Vision in Religion

President Elect Barrack Obama has not even assumed office, yet the pro-life activists have already declared "war" on his administration because of his pro-choice political position. They seem to ignore the results of the election that Obama won 52.7% of the popular vote, received 56% of votes by women, 66% of under age 30 and 68 % of new voters.

The possible signing of the Freedom of Choice Act (FOCA) by President-Elect Barack Obama would be "the equivalent of a war" an unnamed senior Vatican official recently told TIME magazine as was reported on www.lifesitenews.com. The LifeSiteNews.com is a strong advocate of pro-life position on behalf of the right wing Roman Catholics. This group is strongly focused on the issue of abortion to the point that any catholic politician who votes for pro-choice should be denied communion and may face excommunication from the Church. This extremism has reached such a high level that some are advocating that US citizens who voted for Obama should confess their "sins" before they may receive communion. The extreme pro-life advocacy group is being supported by several high ranking leaders of the Roman Catholic Church. For example, speaking at the Catholic University of America after the US election, Vatican Cardinal James Stafford labelled Obama's pro-choice policies as "aggressive, disruptive, and apocalyptic," also noting that, "On November 4, 2008, America suffered a cultural earthquake". John-Henry Westen, Editor-in-Chief of LifeSiteNews.com stated that with Catholic pro-abortion individuals occupying two prominent positions in the Obama administration (Joseph Biden as vice president and Tom Daschle as Health and Human Services Secretary), the possibility of public excommunication or denial of communion has arisen. Westen further reported that at the mid-November meeting of US Bishops in Baltimore, Cybercast News Service asked Chicago Cardinal Francis George, the current president of the U.S. Conference of Catholic Bishops, if voting for FOCA would bring a penalty of automatic excommunication for Catholic politicians. The Cardinal did not rule it out. "The excommunication is automatic if that act is in fact formal cooperation, and that is precisely what would have to be discussed once you would see the terms of the act itself," responded Cardinal George. When asked for more, he added: "The categories in moral theology about cooperating in evil, which make you complicit in the evil even though you don't do it yourself, are material cooperation, which is usually remote and therefore doesn't involve you in the moral action except in a very auxiliary and minor way, and formal cooperation, which would involve you even though you are not doing it, in the way that makes you culpable. In a message to the Obama Administration at the end of the USCCB meeting George wrote on FOCA, saying it would, "outlaw any 'interference' in providing abortion at will. It would deprive the American people in all fifty states of the freedom they now have to enact modest restraints and regulations on the abortion industry". The Cardinal added: "FOCA would have an equally destructive effect on the freedom of conscience of doctors, nurses and health care workers whose personal convictions do not permit them to cooperate in the private killing of unborn children. It would threaten Catholic health care institutions and Catholic Charities."

Tony Perkins of the Family Research Council said that the appointment of Tom Daschle gives pro-lifers a "frightening glimpse" into the new Cabinet. According to Perkins, the former Democratic Senate majority leader Tom Daschle gained notoriety for his liberal views on abortion when he opposed the partial-birth abortion ban, endorsed taxpayer-funded military abortions, and supported taxpayer funding to provide morning-after pills to young public school girls. This pro-life advocacy group was further angered by the possible appointment of Arizona governor Janet Napolitano as Obama's secretary of Homeland Security. According to Kathleen Gilbert of LifeSitenews.com Janet Napolitano, an early Obama supporter, firmly established herself as an extreme abortion supporter by vetoing the partial birth abortion ban, and in one month she vetoed four anti-abortion bills. The possible appointment of Hilary Clinton as Secretary of State is also viewed by this group as another indication that President Elect Obama is stacking the decks with pro-choice Cabinet members.

The pro-life advocacy groups is equally concerned that Mr. Obama is quickly establishing his public solidarity with the homosexual movement. They claim that Obama recently laid out on his website a "civil rights agenda" that includes, to the satisfaction of homosexual lobbyists, the dismantling of legal protections for marriage. He intends to repeal the Defense of Marriage Act, the act that protects natural marriage that is currently enshrined in federal law, and accordingly opposes a federal Constitutional amendment to protect marriage. A further concern is that Obama has also promised to expand "hate crime" enforcement and legislation by enacting the Matthew Sheppard Act, which would allow a perceived bias against homosexuality to be prosecuted. Obama will also enforce non-discrimination in businesses regarding homosexuality.

However, the strong views of the pro-life group as featured on LifeSiteNews.com is not supported by many (or even the majority of) Catholics. For example, California's first lady, Maria Shriver, recently told Sally Quinn of the Washington Post that she considers herself "a Catholic in good standing". On the disparity between Church teaching and her belief on abortion, Shriver told Quinn, "I often talk to my daughters at the dinner table about the difference between being pro-abortion and being pro-choice." She explained that she believes supporting the right to choose an abortion is different from supporting abortion. California's first lady Maria Shriver also pointed out her disagreement with the Church on the issue of homosexuality. She said she does not believe that "people who are gay shouldn't be accepted into the church." However, while the Catholic Church teaches that all sexual activity outside of marriage, including homosexual activity, is sinful, there is no prohibition against people with homosexual inclinations being welcomed into the Church. The Church strongly recommends loving acceptance of such persons and spiritual direction and other assistance to help them live faithful Catholic lives.

California Gov. Arnold Schwarzenegger stated that "I always said that you should not have your religion interfere with government policies or with the policies of the people," Schwarzenegger said at a Toronto press conference last year, as he advocated research on human embryos. The results of the US election seem to indicate the California governor has a good understanding of the democratic will of the people.

The views and believes of current generation Catholics are best captured by Mary Gail Frawley-O'Dea in an open letter to her bishop, Peter J. Jugis. The letter was posted on www.newcatholictimes.com a website that presents issues in a more balanced manner than the www.lifestylenews.com It is entitled "Dear Bishop: Please become a credible pro-life advocate". Mary Gail Frawley-O'Dea, a clinical psychologist, was the only mental health professional to address the U.S. Conference of Catholic Bishops at their seminal 2002 Dallas meeting on the sexual abuse crisis, and she was one of the clinicians speaking about sexual abuse to the Conference of Major Superiors of Men that year. Frawley-O'Dea is co-author of Treating the Adult Survivor of Childhood Sexual Abuse, and co-editor of Predatory Priests, Silenced Victims.

The letter starts with the chilling impact of the actions of extreme "pro-life" advocates on children and society. She writes: "On Sunday, September 21, I took my ten-year-old daughter and my seven-year-old daughter to the Obama Rally in downtown Charlotte. As we waited for over an hour to enter the rally area, we were confronted with anti-choice protesters, many of them self-identified as Catholics, occupying two corners of Elizabeth Street. The very large posters they held depicted what they claimed to be aborted babies. If these photos are real, they show dilation and extraction abortions. The implication, however, was that all abortions resemble the grotesque posters held by the protesters. There was no way to shield the many children waiting in line from viewing these posters. Other signs held by the protesters announced that Obama supported the murder of children and that abortion kills "children." My youngest child was cranky and unwilling to sleep Sunday night. When my husband and I took her into our room, she screamed inconsolably for a long time. When I asked if the baby posters scared her, she began to cry, nodding yes, and curled into fetal position. I explained to my little Sally that people who are trying to offer a simple solution to a complex problem sometimes try to scare people into believing what these people want them to believe. I told her the posters were meant to frighten and shock and I explained that good, decent people do not try to win arguments by scaring others, especially little children. I assured her that Barack Obama has two little girls whom he loves dearly and I told my sweet and innocent daughter that Senator Obama would never try to hurt her or any other little children. Having screamed for over an hour, she was asleep in thirty seconds".

In her letter, Gail Frawley-O'Dea brings some facts to the attention of her Bishop, i.e., "89% of all American abortions occur during the first 12 weeks of pregnancy when no life could possibly be sustained outside the womb; 0.2 percent take place 21 or more weeks into a pregnancy, thus representing dilation and extraction abortions. The most common reasons for abortions after 20 weeks are 1. the fetus is already dead in the womb; 2. the fetus has developed anencephaly and will die within five days of birth, and 3. the fetus has severe hydroencephalus, with a skull up to 250% its normal size and therefore dangerous for the mother to continue to carry. Why then are anti-choice posters only demonstrative of the least common, most gruesome abortion procedure?"

Barack Obama has suggested that people from every point on the abortion debate spectrum meet on common ground to reduce the number of abortions in the US. Expanded availability of contraceptives, sensible sex education, expanded resources for women who wish to carry to term and either keep their babies or place them up for adoption, real intervention in poverty, especially for women -- all are ways to reduce the incidence of abortion.

Gail Frawley-O'Dea concludes her letter by saying: "I am not a supporter of all abortions. I would like to see fully funded first trimester abortions available to anyone. Second trimester abortions, in my opinion, should be available only to women who were raped or incested, whose lives are endangered, or who are carrying a damaged child that they simply do not have the emotional, financial, or spiritual resources to care for. Third trimester abortions should be allowed only if the mother's life is in clear and urgent danger. At the same time, I think hysterical and misleading protests that border on the obscene are sinful and divergent from the honesty, integrity, and ultimate compassion of Jesus of Nazareth. Surely, the Church could redirect their ostensibly pro-life advocates to use more representative advertising, to refrain from *ad hominem* and distorted attacks on politicians, and to expand their efforts in directions that support the life of ALL of God's little ones. The Catholic Church would have a heck of a lot more credibility if it seemed as concerned with protecting the born as it does with shaming women who choose to end pregnancies they are not equipped to confront. In the meantime, you can add my daughter to the list of children traumatized by activities sanctioned by the Catholic hierarchy".

As another Roman Catholic in good standing, I am highly critical of the activities of the extreme pro-life activists and strongly support the position of Governor and First Lady Schwarzenegger and that of clinical psychologist Mary Gail Frawley-O'Dea. In addition, I am in disagreement with some of the man-made rules of the Catholic hierarchy, such as discriminating against women by not allowing them to be priests and enforcing celibacy on priests. In many ways the celibacy position brought about the abuses to children by priest, which the extreme pro-life activists conspicuously ignore.

Roadmap to Heaven without a GPS

Some religious leaders claim that they have the best roadmap to Heaven. But, is their GPS working?

Some people live a highly disciplined religious life, believing that through such existence they will go to Heaven, while others have not even been able to come to terms with the definition of Heaven.

While there are different definitions of Heaven documented in various religions and spiritual philosophies, the common denominator appears to equate to the holiest place accessible by people who practice high standards of dignity, goodness, piety and faith. The specific definition of Heaven appears to depend largely on religious traditions. Some religions conceptualize Heaven as some type of peaceful life after death defined in terms of immortality of soul, a place of eternal happiness. There are significant differences among the various religions on the physical location of Heaven, ranging from the sky or high above to a place that has no locational relationship to any planet. Further readings on this topic can be found on http://www.afterlifedata.com/afterlife_sources.php?status=used.

In particular, it is interesting to note Michael Newton's research documented in "Destiny of Souls" that upon death we go directly from one astral plane around earth through the gateway into the spirit world, which is an ethereal space without zones or barriers around it.

Religious leaders seemed to have focused their power of influencing the faithful on the ways they can enter Heaven. One of the fundamental roadmap to Heaven is based on the condition that we must live a "good life" within the terms of a particular spiritual system. Here again, religions differ from strict adherence to the terms documented by spiritual leaders to sola fide (by faith alone) doctrine that asserts that God's pardon to guilty sinners granted to and received through faith or belief alone (http://en.wikipedia.org/wiki/Sola_fide). Some religious leaders in the camp of strict adherence to God's "rules" often focus more on level of control than on showing how to live a good life with dignity, goodness, piety and faith. At times, examples of such actions culminated into holy wars which were military campaigns justified by religious differences. But thankfully, the majority of religious leaders have been able to focus on being good shepherds, believing in God's care for his people, and dedicating their lives to providing a spiritual leadership that helps the faithful to lead a "good life" here on earth and realize eternal happiness after death.

During my personal journey that has provided opportunities to witness life in many part of the world and under different cultures ranging from atheist communism to different religious practices, I came to the conclusion that extreme interpretation of the "good book", be it the Bible, Torah or Qur'an, may not provide the most direct route to Heaven. I also came to realize that Heaven can be found here on earth in the form of happiness. When I look back on my journey, I was happiest when my personal relationships were focused on giving rather than receiving,, when my professional life was directed towards contributing rather than taking, and when I was able to provide service to those less fortunate than I was. These opportunities were not always found through organized religion; I found some through service clubs (37 years in Kiwanis leadership, including District Governor of Kiwanis International) and through being a caring father and grandfather. We can experience "moments of Heaven" here on earth and if we are able to cultivate the right mindset, these moments can become a continuum.

As far as Heaven after death is concerned, I look at it as eternal happiness of my soul, reconciling with God my mistakes on earth and "perhaps" getting a few brownie points for the good deeds. Deep down I kind of hope that my spirit be awarded a special bonus of seeing my children and grandchildren live happy lives.

It is time for Vatican III

While Vatican II addressed a large number of issues, the two most significant dimensions to this ecclesial theme were: understanding the Church in itself and the Church in relation to the world, including its relationship to other Christian traditions, other faiths and secular world (for further information: http://www.vatican2voice.org/4basics/themes.htm). Vatican II spanned two papacies: that of John XXIII who convened the Council and Paul VI who succeeded him and closed it. Although the Popes were significant figures in the proceedings of the Council, they rarely attended the working sessions. Instead they followed proceedings on closed circuit television, or by studying reports of proceedings and drafts of final documents; their interventions are recorded in the Vatican archives. The working members of the Council were the "Council Fathers" (2,500 in numbers) who were mainly of Episcopal (bishop) rank and were entitled to vote and speak in the debates, as well as make written submissions. Each Council Father was entitled to bring a theologian, or other appropriate expert of his choice, who would usually require formal accreditation. These experts played a valuable role in shaping debates and in the ensuing documents. In addition, a number of senior members of other Christian denominations were invited to the Council as observers and they contributed in private discussions only.

The Council succeeded in making a significant number of positive changes in the operations of the Catholic Church (renewal, liturgy, etc), its relation to ecumenism and other religions, and its role in the modern world, . These changes are documented in 4 Constitutions, 9 Decrees and 3 Declarations. Pope John XXIII had a loving vision for the Church and humanity. It is most unfortunate that he died before being able to put into action the recommendations of the Council.

Pope Paul VI is credited with implemented most of the recommendations of the Council. However, the Council did not succeed in addressing two important topics with conclusive recommendations: birth control and priestly celibacy. Many of the bishops wished the Council to consider the matter, but Paul VI insisted on reserving it to himself. In 1967, he issued the Encyclical *Sacerdotalis coelibatus* on priestly celibacy and on 25 July 1968, birth control was the main topic of his Encyclical *Humanae vitae*.

It is interesting to note that Bishop Wojtyła (later Pope John Paul II) participated in all of the assemblies of Vatican II and that he was instrumental in formulating the Encyclical *Humanae vitae* which deals with the issue of abortion and birth control. When Bishop Wojtyła became Pope John Paul II in 1978 he continued to implement the recommendations of Vatican II, as well as strongly supported the Church's position on celibacy and birth control.

It is a sobering reality check that while mandatory celibacy was initially created to protect the wealth of the church, in recent times it has caused some of the wealth to slip away as payments of compensation to those who have been sexually abused by priests. Under voluntary celibacy, the church would have a large number of married priests and the screening of pedophiles would not be impacted (minimized) because of the shortage of priests.

Since Vatican II society has undergone major changes fuelled greatly by the rapidly expanding communications media with Internet being its flagship. To some degree celibacy is responsible for the shortage of priests; added to that is the current position that prevents women from entering the priesthood. Also, the spreading of AIDS is putting pressure on the Church to reconsider its position on birth control and do a reality check on human behaviour. Hence, it is time to get all the Bishops involved in examining these two topics. The Council of Bishops need to be involved in the decision making on celibacy and birth control rather than the Roman Curia that appears to have gained increasing power since Vatican II in terms of influencing the Pope.

Hence, it is time to consider Vatican III.

ABOUT POLITICS

Communism had a cut-throat start

I was in grade 6 when communism was introduced to a country that was just recovering from the Nazi occupation, had a short introduction to socialism, then was on a fast track course to communism a la Stalin.

In school we learned about the virtues of communism. It was branded as the emancipation of the working class, the proletariat. Communism was portrayed as a political system in which there is full equality for all members to participate and share in the benefits of production, it represents a free society with no division or alienation, where humanity is free from oppression and scarcity. In reality, however, the opposite was practiced in many East European countries in the late 1940's and early 1950's largely due to the continuous power struggles among top communist leaders whose main objective was to take control. This was especially true in Hungary.

During World War II, a communist cell headed by Lászlo Rajk, a veteran of the Spanish Civil War and a former student communist leader, operated underground within Hungary. Mátyás Rákosi led a second cell from Moscow. After the Soviet Red Army invaded Hungary in September 1944, Rajk's

49

organization emerged from hiding and the Rákosi group returned to Hungary. Rákosi's close ties with the Soviets enhanced his influence within the party, and a rivalry developed between the Muscovites and Rajk's followers.

Rákosi described himself as "Stalin's best Hungarian disciple" and "Stalin's best pupil." He also invented the term "salami tactics" which related to his approach of eliminating the opposition slice by slice.

In 1946 Rajk organized the Hungarian Communist Party's private army, the brutal secret police (AVH). Under the cover of "struggle against fascism and reaction" and "defense of the power of proletariat", he prohibited and liquidated several religious, national, democrat and maverick establishments and groups.

The communist infighting used anti-Titoism as an opportunity of getting rid of communists who favored national pride, some measure of independence, and especially those who were not trained in the Soviet Union. Rákosi saw Rajk as a threat to his power, so he decided to accuse him on false charges of being an agent of Tito and had him arrested in 1949. Rákosi orchestrated Rajk's show trial mainly to please Stalin who was furious with Tito. Rajk was sentenced to death in a "show trial" and was hanged.

Between 1949 and 1952 Rákosi's regime practiced political cleansing by deporting Hungarian families to forced labor camps. There were 13 such camps which were populated with 2,500 families totalling about 8,000 interns and included besides able bodied men and women, children and senior citizens. These deportations were not decided by any court of law but simply by local communists and the political police. Rákosi imposed authoritarian rule and totalitarian communism on Hungary. An estimated 2,000 people were executed and over 100,000 were imprisoned. These policies were opposed by some members of the Hungarian Workers Party and around 200,000 were expelled by Rákosi from the party.

Those of us who were in high schools and Universities at the time and were subjected to study Marxism and communism, rebelled against the injustices of the authoritarian and undemocratic leadership. The student revolt subsequently expanded into a revolution in October 1956. Although many of us paid the price of losing our homeland, some even their life, the movement against the cut-throat communism was the first major step towards stopping such evil dictatorship.

Communism at Crossroads

Communist dictator Stalin died on March 5, 1953. His death provoked a mixture of grief, relief, and anxiety for the future. With no clear successor evident, the Council of Ministers and the Presidium of the Supreme Soviet publicly declared a form of collective leadership which in turn initiated a bitter power struggle among top contenders. Malenkov was appointed chairman of the Council of Ministers, in effect premier, with Beria as his deputy and chief of state security. Molotov returned as foreign minister and Bulganin became minister of the armed forces. Nikita Khrushchev's name was listed first among the five secretaries of the party secretariat. Malenkov was also appointed first secretary of the Communist Party, which was Stalin's old position, but nine days later he was forced to surrender this post when the new leadership decided that all the top offices should never again be held by one person. Malenkov showed no desire to maintain the culture of repression and fear that were characteristic of Stalin's rule.

After Stalin's death Beria took more direct control of the Soviet nuclear project. Without consulting his colleagues, he ordered scientists to race ahead with developing a hydrogen bomb to rival

America's thermonuclear weapons. Khrushchev became convinced that Beria was preparing to make a grab for absolute power. Malenkov concurred, and he denounced Beria at a meeting of the Presidium. Tainted from heading Stalin's terror apparatus, Beria was arrested in June 1953 on trumped-up charges of being a western agent. Ironically, the man who had sent hundreds of thousands to their deaths was not even allowed to attend his own trial. He was found guilty and shot in December 1953.

Now that Beria was out of the way, Khrushchev was able to replace Malenkov as first secretary of the Central Committee of the Communist Party. During the next two years Khrushchev out-manoeuvred his remaining rivals to emerge as the Kremlin's leading light. Khrushchev denounced Stalin in his "secret speech" before the 20th Congress of the Soviet communist party on February 25, 1956. The 20th Congress of the Communist Party of Soviet Union marked a turning-point in the politics and ideology of the international communist movement. Although Khrushchev's secret speech revealing the crimes of Stalin was not to be published, news of it began to spread immediately after he read it out to party leaders.

The 20th Congress placed insoluble tasks before many Eastern European party leaders. The most conspicuous of these party leaders was Rákosi who a few years ago claimed to be Stalin's best Hungarian pupil. He now had to head the de-Stalinization process, unveil the mistakes and crimes of the past, and condemn the culprits, especially himself. Rákosi was not able to survive this challenge. He was relieved of his main functions on July 21, 1956 on the grounds of ill health. He was exiled to the Soviet Union.

The 1956 Student Revolution

In the summer of 1956, the Soviet leaders decided that the time had come for another political intervention in Hungary. The situation was causing concern not only for the Soviets but throughout the socialist camp where it was feared that unexpected, disagreeable events might occur. The likelihood of this was increased by the demonstrations in Poland, where the security forces used arms to break up workers who were demonstrating for an improvement in living and working conditions. To prevent any similar occurrence in Hungary, Anastas Mikoyan arrived in Budapest with a strong mandate to handle the crisis. Rather than defusing the crisis, Mikoyan's visit ignited further the nationalistic sentiment, especially among young intellectuals.

On October 22nd students at the Technical University in Budapest decided to formulate demands on the Government. This was the first time that any group dared to call communication with the government: "demands". The demands focused on 16 areas some of which were:

1. We demand the immediate evacuation of all Soviet troops;

2. We demand the election by secret ballot of all Party members from top to bottom. These officers shall convene a Party Congress as early as possible in order to elect a Central Committee.

3. A new Government must be constituted under the direction of Imre Nagy: all criminal leaders of the Stalin-Rákosi era must be immediately dismissed.

4. We demand public enquiry into the criminal activities of Mihály Farkas and his accomplices. Mátyás Rákosi, who is the person most responsible for crimes of the recent past, must be returned to Hungary for trial before a people's tribunal.

5. We demand general elections by universal, secret ballot are held throughout the country with all political parties participating.

Such demands shocked the dictatorial communist government. The demands promoted democracy which was not compatible with the way the country run under communist rule.

On October 23rd, the students of the Technical University started a peaceful march to show their support for the Poles, to demonstrate that Hungary wanted to be politically and economically independent, and to end the Soviet occupation. Later that evening the students tried to broadcast their demands at the Hungarian Radio Station. The Radio Building was guarded by a detachment of the secret police called AVH. When the crowd began to threaten the building after a student delegation was detained within, the AVH officers panicked and opened fire on the demonstrators, killing several including women and children. This was the moment when the unrest and frustration of thousands of people turned from peaceful protest to revolution.

The news spread quickly and disorder and violence erupted throughout the capital. The revolt spread across the country, several police stations and army units provided arms for the freedom fighters and the government fell. Thousands organized into militias, battling the secret police (AVH) and Soviet troops. Some communists and AVH members were hanged, shot or imprisoned. Local councils took over municipal control from the Communist Party and demanded political changes. Nagy formed a new government, abolished the AVH and begun negotiations for the complete withdrawal of the Soviet troops. By the end of October, fighting had almost stopped and a sense of normality began to return. Those of us who took part in the student revolution were ready to return to school, celebrating our victory. But on November 4th we were silenced as the

Russian tanks rolled into Budapest to crush the student revolution.

Collapse of Communism in Hungary

In the late 1980's Hungary played a key role in the collapse of Communism in Eastern Europe. It started in early September 1989 when Hungary opened its borders to allow thousands of East Germans to escape to Austria on their way to West Germany. Two months later, the Berlin wall came down.

The road to democracy was initially slow and painful. János Kádár a Soviet loyalist who replaced Imre Nagy as Prime Minister after the defeat of the 1956 revolution declared war on the revolutionaries and was nicknamed the "Butcher of Budapest". But in the early 1960s in an attempt to overcome his popularity challenges, Kádár adopted a new policy under the motto: "He who is not against us is with us" which was a modification of Rákosi's statement "He who is not with us is against us". He also declared a general amnesty on the 1956 "counter revolutionaries", curbed some of the excesses of the secret police, and instituted a platform of national reconciliation. In 1966, he introduced a "New Economic Mechanism," through which he aimed to rebuild the economy, increase productivity, make

Hungary more competitive in world markets, and create prosperity to ensure political stability.

The changes that took place as a result of these economic measures gradually improved the standard of living in all segments of society. I visited Hungary in June 1974 for the first time after escaping in 1956 and one could see improvements in the availability of food and consumer goods. However, the central control of the Government eased very little, although Hungarians were allowed to visit relatives in the West. Former freedom fighters were also allowed to visit relatives in Hungary provided that they stayed away from making any political comments.

The Government gradually realized that these visits brought into the country valuable foreign currency, especially the mighty US Dollar. In major cities special stores opened up selling alcohol, tobacco and national souvenirs for foreigners and payments had to be made with US currency. During my subsequent visits to Hungary (every 2-3 years), I noticed that conditions were improving quite rapidly, lineups for food and other consumer goods were rarely seen and visits of Hungarian citizens to western countries were allowed. During one of these visits I was able to take my sister to Vienna for a day's shopping.

Hungarians nicknamed this new political phenomenon: "Goulash Communism". Goulash is a popular Hungarian dish with assortments of unlike ingredients. This version of communism included elements of free market and improved human rights; it showed a concern for public opinion and an increased focus on the present (rather than future) material well-being of the citizens.

. In October 1989, the communist party convened its last congress and re-established itself as the Hungarian Socialist Party while at the same time the Parliament adopted legislation providing for multiparty elections. The legislation also transformed Hungary from a People's Republic into the Republic of Hungary. Interestingly, the Republic of Hungary was officially declared on October 23rd 1989 which coincided with the 33rd anniversary of the 1956 revolution.

The first free parliamentary election was held in May 1990. The revitalized and reformed communists performed poorly despite having more than the usual advantages of an "incumbent" party. Populist, center-right, and liberal parties fared best. But, in May 1994, the socialists came back to win a plurality of votes. Since 1994, power shifted back and forth but always adhering to democratic principles.

Collapse of Communism in USSR

In terms of chronological events, the collapse of communism in the Soviet Union is blamed on or credited to Mikhail Gorbachev, depending on one's viewpoint.

Upon the death of Konstantin Chernenko, Mikhail Gorbachev, at the age of 54, was elected General Secretary of the Communist Party on March 11, 1985. He became the Party's first leader to have been born after the Revolution. Once he took office, he tried to reform the stagnating Party and the state economy by introducing glasnost ("openness"), perestroika ("restructuring"), demokratizatsiya ("democratization"), and uskoreniye ("acceleration", of economic development), which he launched at the 27th Congress of the Communist Party of the Soviet Union in February 1986.

Gorbachev realized that reforms were needed to improve worker productivity and the standard of living in the Soviet Union. He also realized that the strong arm approach of the Soviet Union over the republics and European satellite countries needed to be relaxed in order to avoid a series of revolutions like those which took place in Hungary and Czechoslovakia. Due to his liberal approach in international relations, Gorbachev was credited with ending the cold war between the Soviet Union and the United States of America and for these efforts he received the Nobel Peace Prize in 1990.

However, domestically Gorbachev's reform programs were increasingly unpopular. In particular, the following programs contributed to the domestic failures of the Gorbachev era.

The first major reform program introduced under Gorbachev was the 1985 alcohol reform, which was designed to fight widespread alcoholism. Prices of vodka, wine and beer were raised, and their sales were restricted. The reform did not have any significant effect on alcoholism in the country, but economically it was a serious blow to the state budget.

The economic policy of Gorbachev's government gradually brought the country close to disaster. By the end of the 1980s, severe shortages of basic food supplies led to the reintroduction of the war-time system of distribution using food cards that limited each citizen to a certain amount of product per month.

The introduction of glasnost was welcomed in general as long overdue, but at the same time opened up desires of "independence" and nationalistic sentiments among individual states in the Soviet Union, as well as among East European states.

Gorbachev attempted to draw up a new treaty of union which would have created a truly voluntary federation in an increasingly democratized Soviet Union. However, the more radical reformists, such as Boris Yeltsin were increasingly convinced that a rapid transition to a market economy was required.

Hardliners in the Soviet leadership launched the August coup in 1991 in an attempt to remove Gorbachev from power and prevent the signing of the new union treaty. During this time, Gorbachev spent three days (August 19, 20 and 21) under house arrest before being freed and restored to power. However, upon his return, Gorbachev found that support had swung over to Yeltsin, whose defiance had led to the coup's collapse.

Between August 21 and September 22, Estonia, Latvia, Lithuania, Ukraine, Belarus, Moldova, Georgia, Armenia, Azerbaijan, Kazakhstan, Kyrgyzstan, Uzbekistan, Tajikstan, and Turkmenistan declared their independence. The presidents of Russia, Ukraine and Belarus met December 8, founding the Commonwealth of Independent States and declaring the end of the Soviet Union. Gorbachev was presented with a *fait accompli* and reluctantly agreed with Yeltsin on December 17, to dissolve the Soviet Union. He resigned on December 25 and the Soviet Union was formally dissolved the next day.

Life after Communism in Russia

Boris Yeltsin played a key role in the collapse of the Soviet Union. He forced Gorbachev to resign as head of the Soviet Union on December 25th 1991 and the once mighty communist empire was dissolved the next day. Yeltsin was a highly popular reformer who criticised Gorbachev for moving too slow towards a free market based economy.

In June 1991Yeltsin received 57% of popular vote in the first democratic presidential election of the Russian Republic. In January 1992 he embarked on a program of radical economic reforms targeted to convert the world's largest centrally controlled economy into a free market one. Some of Yeltsin's advisors favoured a rapid approach for this transition while others argued that a gradual or slower pace would be more suitable under the existing conditions. Not receiving a consensus from his advisors, Yeltsin turned to western economists and institutions, such as the IMF, the World Bank and the U.S. Treasury Department, who had developed a standard policy recipe for transition economies in the late 1980s. This recipe was known as the Washington consensus or shock therapy, was adopted by Poland and was favored by Yeltsin's deputy, Yegor

Gaidar, a 35-year of Russian economist. It contained measures intended to liberalize prices and stabilize the State's budget. As an integral part of implementing the shock therapy, Yeltsin ordered the liberalization of foreign trade, prices and currency while at the same time introduced harsh austerity measures designed to control inflation. In addition, interest rates were raised to high levels, government subsidies to industry and construction were cut, new taxes were introduced and steep cuts were made to welfare spending. In mid 1992, prices skyrocketed throughout Russia, the deep credit crunch shut down many industries and the country experienced severe depression. The radical reforms devastated the living standards of much of the population, especially the groups dependent on Soviet-era state subsidies and welfare programs. Yeltsin's popularity slid to an all time low.

In February 1996 Yeltsin announced that he was planning to seek another term in the 1996 presidential election. But during Yeltsin's first term, the Communist party of the Russian Federation gained more support than the polls predicted for Yeltsin. Fearing the possibility of defeat, Yeltsin's supporters rallied well-connected Russian business leaders by offering them majority stakes in some of Russia's most valuable state-owned assets.

Yeltsin's campaign also got a boost from the announcement of a $10 billion loan to the Russian government from the International Monetary Fund. At the same time the media painted a picture of a fateful choice for Russia, between Yeltsin and a "return to totalitarianism." The business leaders even played up the threat of civil war if a Communist were elected president. As a result, Yeltsin won a second term as president of the Russian Federation. During his two terms Russia received US$ 40 billion from IMF and other international financial institutions. This helped with the transition to free market economy. However, Yeltsin never recovered politically, narrowly missed several impeachment efforts.

On 31 December 1999, in a surprise announcement aired at 12:00 noon on Russian television Yeltsin said he had resigned and Prime Minister Vladimir Putin had taken over as acting president, with elections due to take place on 26 March 2000.

I had several visits to Russia during the Yeltsin era, attempting to do business with Russian private sector companies and government agencies. It was obvious to me that there were some disappointments with the slow progress in the improvements of economic conditions, yet at the same time only a relatively small percentage of the population wished to return to the old communist regime.

Surviving Refugee Life

November 19th 1956 was a pivotal day in my life. I crossed the Austrian border from Hungary, left behind family and the homeland that I loved. At 18 one is supposed to be adventurous, willing to explore new horizons. But, when at age 18 you are away from home for the first time, and in a foreign land where you don't understand the language, live in a guarded camp, the spirit of adventure can become a frightening picture of reality.

The exodus of over 200,000 Hungarians to the west after the defeat of the 1956 student revolution in Hungary created some real challenges to western powers. Governments were genuinely willing to help by taking in refugees but the numbers put a new reality check on the magnitude of willingness. Besides the humanitarian sympathy, there was a feeling of guilt by some countries who encouraged freedom fighters through Radio Free Europe and Voice of America by implying (without actually saying) that help was on its way. We believed them and when help was not coming, we felt abandoned. (In addition, the timing of the French-British-Israeli invasion of Egypt over the nationalization of the Suez canal was

73

considered to be a significant contributor towards the defeat of the revolution.

In the refugee camps near Graz, Austria, delegations of western countries were holding meeting to screen refugees. There was a serious concern by western countries, that members of the dreaded Hungarian secret police also crossed the border and were among us seeking refugee status. Then there was talk that our ranks were infiltrated by communists who's objective was to spy for the Soviet Union. This in turn created suspicion on all refugees and the onus was on us to prove that we were not one of the undesirables.

When the exodus of refugees picked up momentum, the US Government initially set a limit of 6,500 but this number went up to 80,000. Canada welcomed 40,000, Britain took in 22,000, France 13,000 and the rest went to other countries. I ended up among those who went to Britain.

Today, it is estimated that over 35 million men, women and children are either temporarily or permanently exiled from their homes. This is more than the entire population of Canada.

Flashback to refugee life brings back memories that are bittersweet. There were feelings of hopelessness: how will I survive in this strange land without speaking the language, having no education or trade, and without the family to support me? At the same time, there was a glimmer of hope that new opportunities will open up. And, I was one of the lucky ones. A wonderful and carrying family that I met in church in Halifax, Yorkshire (Mr. and Mrs. Gillespie) took interest in my situation. They helped me with learning the English language and invited me for lunch every Sunday after church. They also helped me to win a scholarship at the University of Edinburgh to study science. Nine months after leaving the refugee camp, I was a full time student at the University studying for a B.Sc. degree.

Life in the Colonial Service

. I arrived in Georgetown, British Guiana on December 4, 1961 from England. I was recruited by the British Colonial Office on behalf of FAO (United Nations) to work as Assistant Conservator of Forests in charge of Forest Surveys. My job was to lead a surveying expedition into the jungles each year for 3 months during the dry season with a crew of 45 men for the purpose of collecting ground survey data in support of making forest cover maps.

The period I spent in British Guiana was politically unstable, was marked by strikes, riots, political unrests and racial tensions. The reason for the disturbances was due to the belief by the British and American governments that the newly elected Prime Minister, Dr. Cheddi Jagan, was a Marxist and would lead his country to be another Cuba.

Initially, I found my situation in British Guiana to be uncomfortable. I was a former freedom fighter from Hungary, an anticommunist and now assigned to work with a Government who was branded by the key western powers as communist. But as I got to know some of the Cabinet members of the Jagan Government, they were far from being communist. They were dedicated to free their country from colonial rule and to make living conditions better for its citizens.

My neighbour in Georgetown was Dr. Morrison Sharp, head of the History Department of the newly established University of British Guiana. He was an academic of liberal views and lost his university position in the U.S. during the McCarthy era. He was recruited to come to Georgetown by Prof. Lancelot Hogben, Vice Chancellor of the University of British Guiana. Dr Sharp was a member of a think tank run by Prof. Hogben, advising the Jagan Government on political science issues. I had the privilege of being invited to join this group to give balance to some of their left leading discussions. The members were real intellectual and very compassionate in their ideology. I learned from this group that extremism to the left or to the right is equally destructive, regardless if it is politically or religiously motivated.

Spending 3 years in a country that was in the process of gaining independence from colonial rule was most educational. Although I was recruited by the Colonial Office, I was treated by my local colleagues differently from how they interfaced with those who were career Colonial Service representatives. I was accepted as being part of a technical aid from FAO. Also, my tenure was clearly for a 3 year term. This position gave me an opportunity to watch the developments as colonial rule was coming to an end. I watched with interest the reaction of people who spent a lifetime working in the colonial service; now they had to accept the fact that their privileged lifestyle was over. They were going back to the old country where they will have to adjust to a more modest life styles and jobs. On the other hand, local intellectuals, professionals and business leaders were waiting anxiously for the day when they would control their own destiny. The future looked exciting for them, full of hope and dreams. But in the meantime, the two sides had to co-exist politely and wait for the day that independence will be granted to this relatively small South American country. I felt like a fly on the wall witnessing history in the making.

End of Colonial Rule in Guyana

Cheddi Jagan was the most significant political figure in the history of Guyana for over 55 years. He changed the course of history of this small South American country, first by struggling to liberate it from British colonial rule, then by waging a 28 year long struggle for the restoration of freedom and democracy, and finally by ascending to the Presidency as Guyana's first democratically elected Head of State.

His grandparents went to British Guiana from Basti in Uttar Pradesh, India, as indentured immigrants in 1901 and "bound" to work on sugar plantations for 5 years. Hard manual labour, poor pay and rough treatment by overseers was the way of life on the sugar estates in those days. Both his parents worked long hours under these conditions with modest return for their hard labour. Young Cheddi Jagan was a good student and with some major sacrifices by his parents he managed to get an education which was remarkable considering the circumstances. In 1935 he graduated from the prestigious Queens College, Georgetown where most of the students came from well to do families. Then in 1942 he graduated with a Doctor of Dental Surgery

(DDS) at the Northwestern University Dental School, Chicago, while at the same time earned a B.Sc. degree at the Central YMCA College. In 1943 he married Janet Rosenberg of Chicago. The seven years he spent in the United States transformed him from someone with a romantic view of politics, an interest in the writings of Gandhi and the independence movement in India (the land of his grandparents), into a Marxist. After graduation he returned with his wife to British Guiana and practiced dentistry. The couple were active in the labour movement and in 1950 organized the Peoples Progressive Party (PPP) party which was aligned to some extent to Marxist philosophy and strongly focusing on independence.

On August 21, 1961 the PPP won the general election with a decisive majority. The two main opposition parties were the Peoples National Congress (PNC) lead by Forbes Burnham and the United Front (UF) under the leadership of Peter d'Aguiar. PPP won 20 seats, PNC 11 and UF 4. Cheddi Jagan was asked to form the government and was designated Premier. On October 25, 1961 Dr. Jagan met with President John F. Kennedy in Washington. On December 18, 1961 he addressed the 4th Committee of the United Nations calling for the British Government to decide on a date for

Independence. But, the British Government refused to grant independence to British Guiana while the PPP was in power even though it had been previously agreed that the party that won the 1961 elections would lead the country to Independence.

Why Jagan was prevented in fulfilling his destiny of leading British Guiana to independence as the country's first democratically elected Prime Minister? Those of us who lived in British Guiana at that time were receiving conflicting answers to this question. The main reason given by the British Colonial Office was because of civil unrests, strikes, riots, looting and racial tensions. The PPP supporters on the other hand claimed that the unrests were orchestrated by the CIA because the Kennedy administration did not want British Guiana to emerge as another Cuba. As we look back on the historical events that were unfolding in British Guiana in the 1960's, mistakes were made by all sides.

Dr. Jagan's passion for independence, social and economic justice made him aggressive in his struggle to bring about change which made the right wing opposition, as well as the British and American governments nervous. He published newspaper articles that were critical of the US interference in Cuba and of the colonial domination. When Cheddi Jagan went to the United States in late October 1961, he failed to make a good impression on President Kennedy. His refusal to say anything negative about the Soviet Union during an appearance on "Meet the Press" angered the President because it made cooperation politically difficult. Other US politicians such as Secretary of State Dean Rusk warned the President that Jagan could become another Castro. Historical documents such as Arthur M. Schlesinger's memoir of the Kennedy White House: "A Thousand Days," and an article published in the New York Times: "A Kennedy-CIA Plot Returns to Haunt Clinton" by Tim Weiner (October 30, 1994) strongly suggest that the President authorized the CIA to work towards the removal of Jagan from power.

I lived in Guyana between December 1961 and December 1964 and witnessed the political turbulences that were taking place at the time. On February 16th, the riots started. Opposition activity began very early on the morning of Friday 16 February in Water Street. Leaders and supporters of the UF encouraged people gathered there to go to the Parade Ground where D'Aguiar would address them. While that meeting was going on a small crowd gathered outside the electricity plant in Kingston and they threw stones and bottles at the windows of the building. The plant was being manned by supervisory staff after the TUC President, Richard Ishmael, had refused the manager's plea that a skeleton staff should be left on duty. The TUC President had demanded that the electricity plant be completely shut down even though fire control in Georgetown depended on water pumped through the mains by electricity. Meanwhile, because of threats on the lives of the skeleton crew at the electricity plant, the members of the supervisory staff were forced to close it down, thus leaving the city without water. During that morning, small fires were already being set by opposition elements in various parts of the city and the Fire Brigade, hampered by the lack of water, was experiencing difficulty in putting them out. From about 1.00 pm the unruly mob, after failing in their attack on Freedom House (headquarters of the PPP), went on a rampage burning and looting business places owned mainly by Indians in Robb, Regent, High, Camp and Water Streets and the Stabroek Market. The fires went out of control because there was no water in the mains; the mob also interfered with the work of the Fire Brigade, even sabotaging its work by cutting the hoses. Water was restored after 5.00 pm when the electricity plant was put back into operation. But by that time the damage was done. There was strong evidence at that time that these disturbances were orchestrated by the CIA with full cooperation from American Institute for Free Labour

Development and with the support of TUC President Richard Ishmael.

The riots gave a reason to the British Government to delay independence. Then in 1963 the British Government changed the electoral system to proportional representation which favoured the opposition. During the December 1964 elections the PPP received enough votes to form a minority government, but the opposition agreed to work out an alliance and were asked to form a coalition government by the British Governor. Once Jagan was out of power, independence was granted to British Guiana and the country's name changed to Guyana. Forbes Burnham ran the country for the next 20 years with force, suspension of freedom and fraudulent elections. He ran up a foreign debt of more than $2 billion, a sum more than five times Guyana's gross domestic product.

In 1992, in the country's first free elections in three decades, Dr. Jagan was elected President, a post he held with honour and distinction as a respected statesman, until his death in 1997.

Arthur Schlesinger Jr. whose "Thousand Days" offers the best-known account of the Kennedy-Jagan encounters said that the classified documents on the CIA activities should be released, so history can be revised. Mr. Schlesinger acknowledged that the US misunderstood the whole struggle in British Guiana at that time and was misled by Burnham.

The full story, he said, proved the truth of Oscar Wilde's witticism: "The one duty we owe to history is to rewrite it".

US "Helped" Castro to Stay in Power

January 1st marked the 50th anniversary of the Cuban Revolution, when the U.S.-backed government of military dictator Gen. Fulgencio Batista was defeated in 1959 by Fidel Castro. US-Cuba relations became strained within a few years to the level that Castro's overthrow was seriously attempted by special interest groups in the US. Yet, Fidel Castro survived and ruled Cuba for 49 years and became one of a few communist dictators who was able to "retire" from his position. How did Castro manage to stand up to the world's most powerful nation for so long? Well, the answer to this question has a historical perspective.

Fidel Castro, a son of a landowner, went to Havana University and graduated with a law degree. During his student days, he got involved in politics and according to him: "One day a copy of the Communist Manifesto- the famous Communist Manifesto! - fell into my hands and I read some things I'll never forget... What phrases, what truths! And we saw these truths everyday!" He ran for the Cuban House of Representatives but troops led by Batista stopped it and exiled Castro to Mexico. In 1956, Castro and about 80 others invaded the Cuban government; they were crushed but escaped into the mountains. In 1957, Castro's forces waged guerrilla wars against the Cuban Government. Finally in 1959 Batista resigned and fled the country. Castro's forces took control of the Cuban government and Castro became the new dictator. He then set out to change ties with the United States: Castro wanted Americans out of Cuba which resulted in bad ties with the United States. The US government became increasingly concerned by Cuba's agrarian reforms and the nationalization of US owned industries. On September 4 1959, US Ambassador Bonsal met with Cuban Premier Fidel Castro to express "serious concern at the treatment being given to American private interests in Cuba both agriculture and utilities. As the reforms continued, trade restrictions on Cuba increased. The U.S. stopped buying Cuban sugar and refused to supply Cuba with much needed oil, with a devastating effect on the island's economy. Each time the Cuban government nationalized American properties, the U.S. government took countermeasures, resulting in the prohibition of all exports to Cuba on October 19, 1960. Consequently, Cuba began to consolidate trade relations with the Soviet Union. In 1961 Cuba resisted an armed invasion by about 1,500 CIA trained Cuban exiles at the Bay of Pigs. President John F Kennedy's complete assumption of responsibility for the venture proved to be a further propaganda boost for the Cuban government. Fidel Castro's enduring tactic has been to fit each initiative to his revolutionary script of a brave Cuba resisting the giant United States. Attempts to bring down the regime in reality even strengthened it. Efforts to democratize Cuba left freedoms further restricted.

As relations deteriorated between U.S. and Cuba, Castro accused Washington of reneging on immigration promises, and threw open the port of Mariel. More than 120,000 refugees landed on Florida's shores, backing the United States into taking them all. This, along with the relatively steady arrival of refugees from Cuba to the United States, gradually changed the dynamics of foreign and domestic policy in the U.S. What started out to be anti-Castro foreign policy gradually became U.S. domestic policy by the fact that some of the U.S. Presidents needed the Florida vote to be elected. For example, in 2000 and 2004, George W. Bush relied on the Cuban vote to carry Florida by narrow margins.

The most significant precondition for improved U.S.-Cuban relations, has taken place not in Cuba, but in the United States, with the November 2008 presidential election. Where past presidents have been beholden to anti-Castro Cuban-American voters in Florida, President Obama proved he could win an election without the previously critical voting bloc. Hence, he has an opportunity of re-establishing U.S. foreign policy independent of the domestic pressures.

President Obama has another opportunity of making history by guiding the U.S. to lift the trade embargo on Cuba. For nearly a half century the U.S. trade embargo on this small and poor country has failed to achieve its intended objectives, i.e., the fall of the Castro regime; the reversal of key domestic Cuban policies; the return of properties belonging to US citizens and firms; and, the severance of the Soviet-Cuban alliance.

Supporters of the trade embargo in the U.S., especially the Cuban exiles and right-wing republicans, focused on toppling the Castro regime at all costs, even at the expense of the ordinary citizens of Cuba who ended up being hurt by it far more than the Government elite. For 49 years Fidel Castro remained in power, using partly the U.S. trade embargo as a justification of his communist dictatorship, as well as for getting aid from the Soviet Union and from other left leaning countries.

The trade embargo also failed to reverse key domestic Cuban policies. The advocates of the trade embargo did not learn from the developments that were taking place in Eastern Europe in the 1980's.

For about 10 years prior to the fall of communism in Eastern Europe, former exiles and refugees were able to visit their relatives in their former homeland without restrictions and were allowed to help them financially. People from these countries were also allowed to visit their relatives in the west and could see first hand that the negative communist propaganda about life in the west was grossly misleading. So changes in the Eastern European communist countries were taking place from within, weakening gradually the grip of communist dictatorship on the ordinary citizens.

The objective of trying to reverse the nationalization of the properties of U.S. citizens and firms was highly unrealistic and shown again a lack of global reality check. Finally, the severance of Cuban-Soviet relations came to an end with the fall of communism in the Soviet Union and the embargo had nothing to do with that. Yet, during the Bush administration, the conditions around the embargo did not ease and in some cases got even tighter.

Now that the U.S. has elected a new President who did not have to rely on the Cuban vote to carry Florida and that he is free of the influence of the conservative republicans who seemed to have been the strong force behind the embargo, there is a unique opportunity to make positive policy changes. Given the setting that Fidel Castro has stepped down as President and is gravely ill, most of the population lives in poverty, and young Cubans would welcome to live in an environment with less restriction on freedom, the time is right for action.

During his campaign for Presidency, Obama said that he intended to remove restrictions on travel and remittances to Cuba by Cuban-Americans and that he favoured well-prepared "direct diplomacy" with the island's communist government. The Obama administration noted with interest recent remarks both by Cuban President Raul Castro and by his brother, former President Fidel Castro, expressing positive sentiments about Barack Obama and the significance of his presidency.

Raul Castro is the younger brother of Fidel Castro. He was an active participant and a Commander in the Cuban revolution. He was appointed Minister of the Revolutionary Armed Forces when the Ministry was founded in October 1959 and served in that capacity until February 2008. He is also the nation's highest ranking general. Raul Castro is credited with persuading his older brother Fidel in the early 1990s, after the Soviet Union collapsed and its generous subsidies to Cuba stopped, to implement agricultural market reforms which increased the food supply for the population. On July 31, 2006, Fidel Castro provisionally handed over the duties of

President of the Council of State of Cuba, First Secretary of the Communist Party and Commander-in-Chief of the Armed Forces to Raul Castro while Fidel underwent intestinal surgery. On February 24, 2008, the National Assembly elected Raul president of Cuba.

Since assuming the presidency Raul Castro's government has announced several economic reforms. In March 2008, the government removed restrictions against the purchase of numerous products, including DVD-players, computers, rice cookers, and microwaves. In an effort to boost food production, the government turned over unused state-owned land to private farmers and cooperatives and moved much of the decision-making process regarding land use from the national level to the municipal level. In 2008, the government overhauled the salary structure of all state-run companies so that harder-working employees could be rewarded with higher wages. In addition, the government has removed restrictions against the use of cell phones and is investigating loosening travel restrictions on Cubans.

There are strong indications that Raul will likely emulate the early phases of the "Chinese model", cautiously opening-up the economy while maintaining strict political control. He may also extend Cubans' ability to work for themselves in modest ways, running hostels, private restaurants or driving their own taxis, but he is unlikely to remove restrictions on things like travelling abroad or forming political parties. However, in order to succeed, he would probably need to see some relaxation of the 46-year-old US trade embargo. Whereas Fidel harnessed anti-American sentiment to rally Cubans and maintain his grip on power, Raul may see benefits in a more accommodating position towards the U.S. Raul Castro seems to be aware that he needs to raise the standard of living for the Cuban populations and tourists spending international currency in Cuba, including U.S. dollars, may turn out to be the most appropriate interim solution to the existing poverty that the Fiedelista political regime ended up with.

The time is right for U.S. President Barack Obama to make some improvements in U.S.-Cuban relations. Lifting the embargo and easing travel restrictions for U.S. citizens on Cuban travel may be the best initial approach. A visit by the American President to Havana may even start an Obamamania in Cuba like it did on February 19th in Canada. However, it is critical for the U.S. to realize that changes to the political system in Cuba will need to come from within the country. The international community has a timely opportunity to create conditions that will be conducive for the changes to evolve. In particular, there must be a delicate balance between the people wanting the changes and the Cuban government allowing them to happen. Raul Castro will not likely to allow as massive changes to happen in Cuba as what occurred in the 1990's in the former Soviet Union and Eastern Europe.

Knockout Punches in Political Debates?

Before each televised political debate, there are a lot of speculations about the possibility or even necessity of one of the leaders to deliver a knockout punch on his/her main rival. This was also the case before the recent Election 2008 debates. If anyone needed to perform in this area, it was Stephane Dion.

Knockout punches seem to work only if a party or its leader has lost confidence of a large segment of voters through their policy, actions or a poorly run campaign. That was the case during the 1984 televised debate. Prior to the debate Liberal Party leader John Turner made a number of "gaffes". In particular, he spoke of creating new "make work programs", a concept from the 1970s that had been replaced by the less patronizing "job creation programs". He also was caught on camera patting Liberal Party President Iona Campagnolo on her posterior. Turner tried to defend this action as being a friendly gesture, but many women viewed it as being condescending. But, what made voters enraged the most was the patronage appointments. Pierre Elliott Trudeau recommended that Governor General Sauvé appoint over 200 Liberals to patronage posts just before he left the office of Prime Minister. Although

Turner had the right to advise the Governor General that the appointments be withdrawn, he didn't do so and to make things worse, he appointed another 70 Liberals to patronage posts despite a promise to bring a new way of politics to Ottawa. Hence, the patronage appointments became a major issue during the July 1984 English-language televised debate between Mulroney, Turner and New Democratic Party leader Ed Broadbent. When Conservative Party leader Brian Mulroney confronted Turner about these appointments, the Liberal leader responded that "I had no option" (referring to a written agreement he made with Trudeau). Then, Mulroney went for the kill: "You had an option, sir. You could have said, 'I am not going to do it. This is wrong for Canada, and I am not going to ask Canadians to pay the price." On September 4, 1984 voters responded by electing 211 conservatives (up from 103), 40 liberals (down from 147) and 30 NDP (down from 32) to the Canadian Parliament. The news media called this the biggest knockout punch in Canadian history.

Stephane Dion tried to land a knockout punch on Steven Harper on October 2nd, 2008 during the English-language debate by coining a phrase from one of the most famous televised debates by saying to Steven Harper: "doing nothing is not an option"..

According to the September polls, Conservatives were heading towards a majority government (conservative supports peaked at 42% while liberals went as low as 23%). The tide seems to have changed after the debates. For example, a poll by Nanos on October 2-4 estimated conservative support at 34% while liberals moved up to 30%. There are many factors affecting these changes. In particular, the economic challenges in the US (brought to the front by the recent bailout) and Steven Harper's perceived alliance with George Bush may have started a re-evaluation in the minds of Canadian voters about a conservative majority government. Also, the re-focus by Stephan Dion from Carbon Tax to economic issues may have helped the liberal cause. Within this climate, the attempted knockout punch "doing nothing is not an option" may have created an awareness in Canadian voters that other counties, especially members of the European Union, are concerned about economic issues as influenced by the developments in the U.S.

Well, Stephan Dion did not land a knockout punch in the debates, The Conservatives took 143 ridings, up from 127 in 2006, while Liberals were elected in 76, a drop of 19 seats from the party's standing at dissolution. Bloc Québécois candidates were elected in 50 ridings, while NDP candidates took

37 seats, a gain of seven seats over the last election. Two Independents also held on to their seats.

Political Goodwill

We often read in the news media about politicians of one party accusing their colleagues in another party of committing deeds that are not in the best interest of the general public. The accusations at times turn even personal and the public then wonders if we can trust our elected officials. Well, recently we were treated to several examples of political goodwill which was like a breath of fresh air.

First, the announcement by Prime Minister Stephen Harper (a Conservative) that he appointed former Premier of Manitoba Gary Doer (an NDP) as Ambassador Designate to Washington was an impressive example of political goodwill, as well as a shrewd move in all aspects. This announcement came just a few days after the Prime Minister appointed 9 conservatives to the Senate (conservatives still need 4 more senators to catch up with the liberals). Press coverage in general has been very positive over Mr. Doer's appointment. He has a proven track record of building consensus and is well respected by politicians in Washington. His political philosophy will be a good match to that of President Obama; so Prime Minister Harper scored in the public opinion on both sides of the border.

Next, the show of respect by republicans to former Senator Edward M. Kennedy at the remembrance ceremonies was most impressive. Sen. Kennedy was diagnosed in May 2008 with malignant brain tumor, fought a courageous battle with this terminal cancer till August 25, 2009 when he died in his home surrounded by his loving family. At a private ceremony on Friday, August 28th several prominent republicans paid tribute to Sen. Kennedy in a rather affectionate manner; as a liberal democrat, he was a strong adversary who reached out to republicans to build consensus when it was required to pass an important legislature in the public interest. He was respected and praised for playing a major role in passing over 300 laws that moved the United States towards an economically more just society, including laws addressing immigration, cancer research, health insurance, apartheid, disability discrimination, AIDS care, civil rights, mental health benefits, children's health insurance, education and volunteering. His most passionate cause was the enactment of universal health care, for which he fought to the end and gave strong support to President Obama. Some democrats are hoping that respect for Sen. Kennedy may be of help to the Obama health reforms so even in death the liberal lion of the Senate could be making an impact in the interest of those economically struggling to survive.

One of the prominent republican senators who paid tribute to Sen. Kennedy was Orrin Hatch ((R-Utah) who considered his liberal adversary a good friend with whom he enjoyed mutual respect. Sen. John McCain (R-Arizona) also spoke affectionately on Friday at the private ceremony in the John F. Kennedy Presidential Library about his friend and colleague, stating that the senator from Massachusetts has brought together political rivals in death as in life; this time to celebrate his life and half a century of service to his country. Sen. McCain referred to Sen. Kennedy as the "best ally you could have" when they agreed on issues and Orrin Hatch said that he said he'd battled like a brother with Kennedy for 33 years and "loved every minute of it."

Finally, it was also re-assuring that the Roman Catholic church was able to overcome their sensitivity with regards to Sen. Kennedy's pro-choice position and his funeral mass was officiated by 10 priests along with Cardinal O'Malley, Archbishop of Boston. Even this dignified religious ceremony can be considered "political goodwill".

Minority Governments

On October 14th 2008 Canadian voters elected another minority Government under the Conservative banner led by Stephen Harper. One of the greatest advantages of the democratic system is that voters have the opportunity of re-aligning the ambitions of political leaders for the better. This seemed to have happened during the recent federal elections in Canada.

Stephen Harper run an excellent campaign, almost cruised to majority, but the international economic crises cautioned the voters to go for checks and balances. Although the conservatives gained 16 seats from the time of dissolution, they came short by 12 seats of winning majority. The Liberals on the other hand, had a tougher challenge. Their leader, Stéphane Dion, could not deliver his vision about the environment and the benefits of carbon tax. Voters in general were not convinced that such a tax would not be passed onto them as an additional burden, especially at a time when gasoline prices went well over a dollar per litre. In addition, the liberal leader's green shift concept muddied the waters of the "reality" that carbon tax is a necessary evil that would help curb harmful emissions. So the liberal standings in the house dropped from 95 at the time of dissolution to 76. So we ended up with another minority government.

During the history of Canadian politics, there have been 11 minority governments at the federal level. In a minority situation, governments must rely on the support of other parties to stay in power. At the federal level no minority government has lasted a standard four-year term. Most minority governments have lasted less than two years. The average duration of a minority Parliament in Canada is approximately 1 year and 4 months.

The first minority government under the leadership of William Lyon Mackenzie King was elected in Canada in 1921 (1 seat short of majority) and lasted for 3 years and 244 days. Actually, this was not a minority government throughout its term because in December 1922 two Progressive members crossed the floor which gave the Liberals majority. The Liberals under King were re-elected again in 1925 as a minority government with reduced confidence of the voters, being 23 short of majority and lasted for 204 days. In the midst of the King-Byng Affair, Conservative leader Arthur Meighen was asked to form a Government (8 seats short of majority but had 15 more seats than the Liberals) which only lasted for 88 days. John Diefenbaker led two minority governments, the first one was elected in 1957 (22 seats short of majority) and lasted for 294 days and the second one was elected in 1962 (17 short of majority) and lasted for 304 days.

I came to Canada in February 1965 at the time when Canada had a Liberal minority government (short by 5 seats), lead by Lester B. Pearson, which was elected in 1963 and lasted 1 year and 182 days. On November 8th 1965 Canadians voted again for another Liberal-led minority government (short of majority by 2 seats), again led by Prime Minister Pearson and lasted for 2 years and 230 days. These two minority governments have been judged by many as the most productive ones in Canadian history. Prime Minister Pearson and NDP leader Tommy Douglas were able to establish a close working relationship, which resulted in the introduction of Canada's health care system (or Medicare), the Canadian Flag and the Canada Pension Plan.

In 1972 the Liberals under Pierre Elliott Trudeau came to power with 23 seats short of majority and lasted for 1 year and 221 days. In order to get the support of the NDP to stay in power, the Liberals had to agree for the creation of Petro-Canada among other things. In 1979 the Conservatives under the leadership of Joe Clark came to power with 6 seats short of majority but lasted only for 273 days when a non-confidence motion was introduced by Bob Rae of the NDP (at that time) and supported by the Liberals.

In 2004 the Liberals under Paul Martin formed a minority government with 20 seats short of majority and lasted for 1 year and 125 days. In 2006 the re-vitalized Conservative party under the leadership of Stephen Harper formed a minority government with 30 seats short of majority, but still managed to survive for 2 years and 256 days. In the 2008 general election, the Conservatives received a better support from the voters (12 seats short of majority) and are expected to last again for over 2 years while the Liberals will be going through the election of a new leader and a re-vitalization process

Election of a Party Leader

On Monday, October 20th 2008, Stephane Dion announced that he was stepping down as leader of the Liberal Party once the replacement is selected. The fact that he chose not to step aside right away and let an interim leader guide the party until a new leader is chosen surprised a large number of people, including many liberals. Dion said that the problems of the party go beyond leadership and he cited party fundraising as one great hurdle to Liberals' election hopes. He noted that the well-financed Conservatives were able to spend "massive" amounts on advertising slamming Dion and the Liberals' carbon tax plan. "We cannot allow others to distort and confuse just because they have more money," Dion said.

This reminded me of the story about General Custer when he saw the Indian braves closing in on him, he apparently turned to his aid and asked: "Who the hell got them mad anyways, last night they were all dancing?"

The question now is: "Who could lead the Liberals back to power?" The Conservatives faced a similar dilemma after the 1993 election when they lost to the liberals and didn't even make it as official opposition. It took them 13 years to get back into a minority government status.

The next question is: "What qualifications and talents should the Liberals set as criteria for the election of the new leader?" This is a similar process as filling a position where there are "must have" and "desirable" qualifications that a candidate needs to have, as well as the need to impress the interview board in order to end up as the most qualified applicant for the job. In that process, it is of critical importance that the interview panel goes beyond their likes and dislikes relative to the candidate and make a decision on the bases that the chosen candidate will have a high probability of succeeding in all aspects of the job.

In order to try to come up with answers to these questions, I went back in history to the time I arrived in Canada (1965) and looked at party leaders from the perspective of what impressed the electorate to choose them to be elected and re-elected as Prime Minister and what led to rejection.

First, successful party leaders excelled in popularity, projecting an image of representing the interests and wishes of most of the people (at that time) through their policy and election platform. They were able to articulate their program in a clear manner and impressed the electorate of their statesmanship. Diplomacy also played a key part in this public relation image, to be respected within the party, in Canada, as well as internationally. Leaders who stood out in this area included Lester B. Pearson (throughout his carrier), and Brian Mulroney (during the first term) and Pierre Elliot Trudeau (often but not always).

Second, successful leaders exhibited strong leadership skills, which they were able to utilize for the benefit of the country's economic performance. Prime Minister Jean Chrétien was highly successful in this area.

Third, an important ingredient of success was vision with charisma. Pierre Elliot Trudeau was the most successful one in this area, especially during the 1968 election when his personal charm and charismatic ways of delivering his message was referred to as Trudeaumania.

Fourth, past successful leaders had the ability to understand the issues that were important to most of the voters and the capability of formulating a policy that would deliver solutions to the challenges faced by the nation. Prime Ministers who excelled in this are since I have been living in Canada included Lester B. Pearson, Brian Mulroney, Pierre Elliott Trudeau, Jean Chrétien, and Stephan Harper.

Rejection or short tenure greeted those party leaders who put their own strong agenda ahead of what the majority of voters wanted. They lacked peripheral vision and stubbornly stuck to their guns that they knew what was best for Canada. This latter approach was exhibited even by some of the successful leaders, especially during their second term of office. As a result, some of the party leaders never got to be prime ministers or those who did, opted for retirement soon after defeat.

In conclusion, it is important to recognize that party members who have the delegated authority of choosing the next leader, bear the ultimate responsibility to the success of their party. Liberals are hoping that the new crop of delegates will do a better job than those who were voting in 2006 when a back room deal by one of the leadership hopeful took out the two star candidates, one of them may have become Prime Minister by now.

Are Democratic Rights Absolute?

Democracy is a form of government in which power is held by people under a free electoral system. Even though there is no universally accepted definition of democracy, there are two principles that any definition of democracy includes: first is that all members of the society have equal access to power and the second that all members enjoy universally recognized freedoms and liberties. In Canada, democracy is further guided by the *Canadian Charter of Rights and Freedoms,* which guarantees the rights and freedoms set out in it subject only to such reasonable limits prescribed by law as can be demonstrably justified in a free and democratic society.

Many Canadians in the Capital region have recently been subjected to a strike by the transit workers. An important element of the democratic right of the transit workers is the right to strike. This means withholding the operations of buses in the greater Ottawa area. On the other hand, people living in Ottawa have the right to use the transportation infrastructure being paid for by the municipal tax payers. In fact, some of the tax payers do not use the facilities they pay for but want to make sure that those who need it can rely on it. When the union leaders of the bus drivers blatantly ignore the damage they cause to their clients and to the local business community, it is time to ask the question: "are democratic rights absolute?" There are many examples in history that democratic rights of one group had to be curtailed to protect the rights of another group. This is definitely the situation at hand as far as the transit workers' strike is concerned.

So following the democratic process, the employers of the transit system, as well as the taxpayers, have the right and responsibility to deliver the service to its citizen in a responsible manner. Senior citizen should not be deprived of this essential service. University students have the right to use the transportation system, especially during the time they are writing their exams. People who have no cars and other transportation system should not be put in a position that they may lose their job and livelihood by another group who have their jobs secure but want to make their situation more comfortable. Elderly people should not be put in harms way when seeking medical attention or even buying groceries by a group that fails to see the reality of our current economic situation. Canada should never be embarrassed again by a group of people by withholding transportation services in the capital city at the time that the world is invited to watch the best in junior hockey.

So, it is time to look for solutions. Settling the strike is the responsibility of the Ottawa city council, headed by a mayor who has established impressive credentials in the business world. At the same time, it is the right of the municipal taxpayers to provide feedback to city council about the transit system and the current strike. A brief survey of a representative section of tax payers formulates the following recommendations:

1. In order to avoid another situation in the future when union leaders of the transit system can hurt their employer and clients as they did during this strike, the Ottawa transit system should be declared essential services, where future disputes would be settled by binding arbitration.

2. Introduction of competition to the Ottawa transit infrastructure should be explored, including full scale privatization.

Mosaic of Canadian Cultures

On Saturday, September 6th 2008 my wife and I had the honour to attend the Annual Gala of the Indo-Canada Ottawa Business Chamber (ICOBC). This was the 3rd consecutive annual gala that we have been invited to. Besides the wonderful company and good food, the gala offered for me, in particular, a nostalgic journey over time starting in 1957.

In September 1957 I arrived in Edinburgh, Scotland to start a B.Sc. program. I was given accommodation at Manor Club, an international youth hostel. I was assigned to share a room with a fellow student from New Delhi, Yatendra Dixit. We soon became best friends and Yatendra introduced me to the fine Indian cuisine that I still love and some of the culture from his home land that he was so proud of.

In February 1965 I came to Canada as a landed immigrant. I was eager to integrate into this new society in the land of opportunities. Since that time, I have travelled extensively around the world visiting many interesting countries and cultures, but each time I land on a return flight to my chosen country, I have a warm feeling of belonging. I have been fortunate to be able to visit the country of my birth, Hungary, several times during the past 40 years and still maintain a connection with my roots through Hungarian cuisine. Most of the time when we entertain I cook Hungarian gourmet meals and look back with pride to my heritage. But, there has never been any question in my mind that my loyalty is now to Canada.

During the gala event I watched with interest Indo-Canadians being honoured for their business and professional success and community service in Canada. As I was reflecting on my association with people from India, I found that we share many common values as new Canadians. Besides the desire to provide a good life for our children and grandchildren and to succeed in business and professional endeavours, we share the desire to pay back for the opportunities this wonderful country has offered us. For the past three years, the annual gala has provided an outstanding show case of these successes; the 15 ICOBC award recipients have all succeeded in their newly adopted country. At the same time they have managed to develop a good practical balance between the rich cultures that they have brought into Canada and their new environment. The injection of new cultures into the Canadian way of life has made this great country the envy of the world in the area of multiculturalism.

As I was listening to the introductions of the award recipients, a new perspective emerged in my mind that is not always emphasized as a benefit of multiculturalism. New Canadians are often involved in building bridges between their old countries and Canada through which mutually beneficial business opportunities and goodwill may travel. This in turn has the opportunity of promoting peace among nations, which is so important in this troubled world of ours.

Yes, on Saturday night I was feeling a great pride of being a new Canadian, celebrating with friends who had similar journeys that brought them to Canada. It is important to show the world that we can practice our cultures and customs in Canada with mutual respect, be proud of our heritage and work together in building a country where future generations will be able to live in peace.

This is the Canadian way!

What the World Needs Now

The Group of Twenty (G20) leaders met for the first time on November 14, 2008, for a working dinner and then on November 15 for a working meeting in Washington D.C. The official name of the meeting was the "Summit on Financial Markets and the World Economy." G20 participants included representatives from Argentina, Australia, Brazil, Canada, China, France, Germany, India, Indonesia, Italy, Japan, Mexico, Russia, Saudi Arabia, South Africa, South Korea, Turkey, the United Kingdom, the United States and the European Union. Spain and the Netherlands also participated in the first meeting as part of the French delegation, under the auspices of the European Union. The second summit is taking place on April 2, 2009 in London, United Kingdom and recommended action items for participants have been compiled by the G20 Research Group (http://www.g20.utoronto.ca/g20plans/g20leaders090327.pdf)

In addition, the British government has set out the following recommendations on what the G20 leaders should focus on at the London Meeting. Key items include that the G20 leaders must reaffirm their determination to stabilize, bolster and reform the financial system, reduce the severity of the global recession and speed up the economic recovery. More action is required to avoid a protracted downturn, guard against deflation, strengthen the financial sector, mitigate against a withdrawal of bank lending and to steer clear of protectionism.

U.S. president Barack Obama and British Prime Minister Gordon Brown are making very public pleas for global cooperation. President Obama calls for the G20 to take "bold, comprehensive and coordinated action" to stem the global economic crisis. The U.S. President calls for action that "not only jump-starts recovery, but also launches a new era of economic engagement to prevent a crisis like this from ever happening again ... Only coordinated international action can prevent the irresponsible risk-taking that caused this crisis". The U.S.'s priorities, however, are opposite of the European members, who want the summit to focus on rewriting rules of governing financial markets. The Europeans believe that bad regulation was a major cause of the crisis and want to tighten their watch over hedge funds and private equity firms.

The document compiled by the G20 Research Group details specific recommendations that leaders of the G20 countries have expressed in an effort to provide solutions for the current economic crisis. It is very reassuring the most of the leaders have put aside self serving and protectionist agendas in order to focus on the stabilization of the global economy.

In addition to the stabilization of the global economy, the world also needs to develop a new culture among some of the top business leaders, especially in the U.S. and Canada, regarding bonuses. While everyday folks have lost substantial amounts of their hard earned investments, many have even lost jobs and pensions, it is unbelievable that top leadership of some of the companies who inflicted these damages feel "entitled" for bonuses in excess of millions of dollars. Whether giving of such bonuses are legal or not, in the opinion of the general public and employees who were laid off without severance pay and pension, they are morally wrong!

When we look back in history, excessive abuses of power have often yielded drastic changes in the political systems of the time. For example, czarism was replaced by communism, capitalist systems were overthrown in favor of socialistic governance, and in some cases the changes went as far as establishing dictatorships. So, let's hope that we can recover from the current economic crises without any threat to our cherished political system: Democracy!

The things I learned from my father

My father grew up in a small village in Eastern Europe. Like many of the people at the time, he had a grade 6 education which was above the village average. He lived through several political systems, including clerical feudalism, Nazi occupation/fascism, socialism, and communism. I also lived under these political systems under his guidance and after leaving the family nest, I had the opportunity of experiencing life under colonialism, capitalism and democracy. I was strongly influenced by father's in depth knowledge of politics.

My father developed rather unbiased and realistic understanding of the various political systems which were controlling life in central Europe during his lifetime.

Under clerical feudalism, the Roman Catholic Church owned a lot of land in Hungary. Our parish priest lived in a mansion, the land under his control produced enough to maintain his rather lavish lifestyle, yet he still demanded donations from villagers, many of whom barely had enough to maintain their modest existence. While father was a supporter of his church and recognized that many were in the priesthood to help the spiritual development of the faithful and the poor, he often warned about the segment of clergy who controlled the land that "they preach water but drink wine".

Father was strong critic of Nazi occupation and fascism. He predicted in the early 1940's that Hitler's Dictatorship will be destroyed and that we may end up living under the war zone. He strongly opposed the Hungarian government's alliance with Germany, even though he was highly critical of the Treaty of Trianon after World War I, which was used as the justification for the Horthy regime to join the Axis powers. He was right in predicting the advancement of the front to our village. Fortunately, he prepared our family for the inevitable. He and grandfather dug a large underground bunker in the barn to store barrels of wines and food supply just in case the soldiers would start looting. He also prepared an underground bunker in the back yard, which came in handy when German and Russian soldiers were fighting door to door in our village. Our family was well protected during the final weeks of war in terms of both safety and food supplies.

Father favoured socialism as a just political system. Unfortunately, it only lasted in Hungary for a few years. He considered communism as a theoretically appealing system which can never work in practice because human beings are competitive in nature. He often said, to the great annoyance of the village priest, that in his opinion, the only person who ever managed to live by the "communist" type of teachings was Jesus Christ. The Church went to acquire wealth, while the communist under Stalin focused on power over people.

I lived under colonialism for three year in British Guiana and was able to observe the end of an era for the same reason that father believed in, i.e., any political system which involves a certain level of exploitation of the less fortunate or of those who oppose it, will ultimately self destruct.

I found capitalism on its own to be a fragile system, but when it is practiced within a democratic framework, it is sustainable.

Unfortunately, father died before the fall of communism in Hungary, so he never been able to live under democracy in his beloved country. But, he came to visit us in Canada five times between 1969 and 1985 and he was happy to witness true democracy in practice.

ABOUT LIFE

The genesis of healthy living

In the early 1960's good living was associated with eating rich and tasty foods such as prime rib with Yorkshire pudding, apple pie with ice cream, lots of wine or beer, followed by a good smoke. In many cultures, if you were slim at age 40, people would ask with some concern: "are you sick?"

The world changed in the 1980's and 1990's. Medical researchers discovered that smoking and eating fatty foods can be hazardous to your health. Over the past 40 years we have been exposed to a wide range of diets, such as traditional, religious, cultural, weight loss, weight gain, weight management, disease fighting, healthy living and individual choice diets. One of the web site on health living lists over 80 different diets which have been invented to guide us towards healthy living. http://en.wikipedia.org/wiki/List_of_diets

While researching the historical development of healthy living, nutrition and diets, I came across a humorous description of lifestyle evolution (author unknown or just simply wouldn't admit to it) which I changed slightly for suitability for this story.

At the beginning, God created the Heavens and the Earth and populated the Earth with broccoli, cauliflower, spinach and Hungarian paprika. So tha' Man and Woman would live healthy lives.

Satan, being jealous of God's goodness, created creamy ice cream, fast food donuts and milkshakes And Satan said to Man and Woman: "you want coffee with that?" Man said "yes" and woman said "make i' double-double for me". They gained 10 lbs and Satan smiled.

God seeing this, offered Man and Woman a healthier alternative: yogurt so that woman can keep the figure that Man found so pleasing. But Satan brought forth white flower, sugar and chocolate-rich desert. And Woman went from size 6 to 14.

Now, God offered again a healthier alternative to Man and Woman and said: "try my fresh green salad". But Satan was determined to win the battle with God so he created Thousand Island dressing, buttery croutons, and garlic toast on the side. And Man and Woman unfastened the belt following the feast.

Then, God created running shoes so that His children might lose those extra pounds. But Satan was quick to the draw and invented cable TV with remote control. Man and woman gained more weight!

Then, God brought forth the potato, low in fat and full of nutrition. But Satan peeled the healthy skin and sliced the starchy center into chips and deep fried them. And Man and Woman gained more weight!

God then created lean beef so that Man and Woman might consume fewer calories and still satisfy their appetite. Satan responded by creating double cheeseburger and deep fried chicken. He then said to Man and Woman: "do you want fries with that, too?" Man said "yes". Satan smiled and Man went into cardiac arrest.

God sighed and created quadruple bypass surgery. Satan responded by creating long line-ups in hospitals and medical centres…

Well, while this may appear to be a fairy tale story, there are some elements of truth to it.

After a bout with prostate cancer, I started to focus on healthy living, including some weight loss. I wanted to increase my energy level and immune system in order to ensure that I beat cancer and be there for the graduation of my grandchildren. A recently published book by Roslyn Franken "The A List: 9 Guiding Principles for Healthy Eating and Positive Living" offered a solutions that I like more than fad dieting: making healthy choices and balancing my servings of various food groups for proper nutrition. By making healthy choices in appropriate proportions, I am losing weight gradually and increasing my energy level to the point that even my highly energetic 4 and 5-year old grandchildren are impressed that Papa can keep up with them.

Transition: middle age to seniors

Middle age is generally considered to occur approximately between the ages of 40 and 60 years. Physical symptoms of middle age include loss of skin elasticity, graying of hair, declines in fitness and increases in body fat. These physical symptoms become more conspicuous after 60 years as adults enter the golden age. As these changes occur, psychological adjustments take various forms, ranging from graceful acceptance of aging to complete denial. The ability to accept the changes that one experiences during such transition appears to be an important ingredient of happiness. While each person has his/her own way of dealing with the changes that occur during the transition, some practices are known to be more successful under different scenarios. Examples of these practices are presented here under their corresponding scenarios.

Scenario: retirement. Some people experience serious difficulties as they face retirement, exhibited in the form of depression, boredom, loneliness and lack of purpose in life. Others get involved in hubbies, volunteer work, physical fitness and social activities. These retirees often say: "I am busier now than I have ever been. I wonder how I had time to work before I retired". These are the happy ones and generally live long enough to enjoy retirement and their pension benefits.

Scenario: facing old age. Some people have difficulty accepting the symptoms of getting older and will try hard to look and act younger, often making absolute fools of themselves. Others, on the other hand, accept old age gracefully without getting frustrated with the reduction in stamina and the changes in the physical appearances. They proudly accept the senior's discounts in stores and dress appropriately. But the most importance sign of acceptance involves scaling down on previous activities and finding happiness in new ventures, such as enjoying a good meal with loved ones and friends, getting involved in social activities appropriate for seniors and focusing on family values. These seniors find happiness in relatively small things and events and appreciate that each day is a new beginning, grateful for the opportunity of being alive and having good health.

Scenario: becoming grand-parents. Some find it difficult to accept reaching the grand-parent stage in life, including having active young ones around who disturb the peaceful afternoons and evenings on the weekends. Others fill their wallets with pictures of the grand children and proud to show them to anyone willing to listen to the stories that they are the most wonderful little people ever been born.

Scenario: personal. I have chosen to deal with the transition from middle age to seniors in my own way. I have accepted with grace that I have put on a few pounds and feel less energetic than I used to feel 20 years ago. I am grateful that professionally I can do assignments much faster than when I was a know-it-all young graduate. So I decided that I will never retire but may slow down after age 80! When I reached 70 I started to use a powered golf cart and changed my focus of getting "exercise" to playing a good game of golf. I am privileged to have 6 grand children, ranging in ages from 5 to 22. I am very proud to admit that I have a grand-son who is a college graduate, I usually qualify the puzzled looks with a statement that I started to have a family when I was only 23. As a grand-parent, I am very lucky. I have the opportunity of looking after the two youngest grandchildren every day for a couple of hours after work. We have fun and I am getting to know these two wonderful young people on a daily basis. I now understand the saying: "If I knew grand children would be this much fun, I would have had them first". I am just a happy senior.

The day I met Dr. Elizabeth Kübler-Ross

In February 1972 I got on an aeroplane in Toronto, heading home to Sault Ste. Marie, Ontario. I was carrying a state-of-the-art (at the time) computer terminal. It fitted into a suit case small enough that I was allowed to carry it on to the plane and put it under the seat in front of me. As I was struggling to fit it under the seat, the passenger next to me watched my predicament with some measure of curiosity. When I finished my ordeal she asked me "what is that?" With a sense of pride I replied: "it's a computer terminal".

As we continued the conversation I explained that I was a research scientist and was building a computer simulation model to illustrate in the computer how trees grow. I then asked her:

"What do you do?" She said:

"I am a writer. I recently published a book called 'On Death &Dying'. I am Elizabeth Kübler-Ross."

Since I was reading mainly technical books and journals at that time, I never heard about her before. So, I continued to put my foot in it. I told her it was pretty gutsy for a writer to take on such a subject. She then smiled and said

"Actually, I am also a medical doctor".

I was interested in the subject matter and we ended up having a good discussion about people's reaction when they are told that they are terminally ill. She explained the five stages patients go through at that time:

Denial and isolation: "not me, it cannot be true"
Anger: "why me?"
Bargaining: "yes me...but"
Depression: "yes me"
Acceptance: "it's OK"

She gave me an autographed copy of her book when I attended her lecture at the Plummer Hospital that evening. I drove her to the airport the next morning and continued to exchange Christmas cards for a few years afterwards.

Thirty two years later I was diagnosed with prostate cancer. On January 27, 2005 I started 37 sessions of radiation treatment in the Ottawa Cancer Clinic. During each session I had to lie on my stomach, the technician strapped a mold on my buttock and the radiation proceeded for about 12 minutes. At that time I often thought of the meeting I had with Dr. Kübler-Ross. I learned to have a deep appreciation of what is now called the "Elizabeth Kübler-Ross model": the five stages of grief as a pattern of phases, most or all of which people tend to go through, not always in sequence, after being faced with the tragedy of their own impending death. While I was determined to survive cancer, I also faced the possibility that my body may not respond to the treatment as expected.

I was one of the fortunate ones thanks to the excellent cancer treatment facilities we have at the Ottawa Cancer Clinic. I responded well and I am now cancer free… as free as one can ever be.

The writings of Dr. Kübler-Ross inspired me to start a similar project after I completed my cancer treatments. This project involved collecting stories of cancer survivors about their reaction and courageous battles after they were told: "you have cancer". I was lucky to have three other cancer survivors to join this project and we have collected heart-warming and emotions packed stories from 36 cancer survivors. We have published these stories in a book called: "Death Can Wait – Stories from Cancer Survivors" by Frank Hegyi, Roslyn Franken, Jacquelin Holzman and Max Keeping.

Kids Say the Darndest Things

One of my favorite TV shows in the 1960's was "Kids Say the Darndest Things" hosted by Art Linkletter from 1952-70. Mr. Linkletter interviewed over 20,000 kids between the ages of 5 and 10 years. The humor was genuine, funny and revealing in terms of what goes on in the minds of young children. For example, he asked one 6 year old boy who was wearing a nice white shirt: "what did your Mummy ask you not to do on the show?" and the reply was "she asked me not to dirty the shirt because we are going to take it back to the store after the show".

Recently I came across some delightful kid's humor, such as:

-JACK (age 3) was watching his Mom breast-feeding his new baby sister. After a while he asked: 'Mom why have you got two? Is one for hot and one for cold milk?'

-MARC (age 4) was engrossed in a young couple that were hugging and kissing in a restaurant. Without taking his eyes off them, he asked his dad: 'Why is he whispering in her mouth?'

-JAMES (age 4) was listening to a Bible story. His dad read: 'The man named Lot was warned to take his wife and flee out of the city but his wife looked back and was turned to salt.' Concerned James asked: 'What happened to the flea?

-MARKY (age 4) told his grandpa that he got a new dog. Then continued to tell him: "Papa my dog was broken but it's OK now because my Dad got him fixed".

Now that I am a grandfather and spend a lot of time with my 4 and a half year old granddaughter (Sara) and 6 year old grandson (Ryan), they remind me of the times Art Linkletter was interviewing the children. The other day Ryan and Sara asked me to take them to Zellers to buy some toys. I said "how about we go to the Dollar Store?" They insisted on going to Zellers where there were toys that they liked better. I said "I don't have enough money to buy expensive toys for you every day". At that point Ryan offered me a solution: "Papa, I can help you if you don't have enough money. Let's go to the bank and put your card in the machine, then press some of the keys and you get money. I will show you how". So we ended up going to Zellers and I bought each of them a toy with my plastic card. Ryan observed the process carefully and commented: "You see it even works here Papa, you don't need money". Afterwards we went for an ice cream and I explained to both of them how the process works.

We live in a fast moving world with technology changes that my grandparents' generation would not have believed possible. When I was Ryan's age, computers and video games did not exist and the most advanced "toy" for me was my father's bicycle (bicycles for kids were not available in our village). It was fun riding the big bike with one leg going under the handle bar to reach the right pedal.

How things have changed! Ryan can turn on my lap top computer, type in the password and gets on the Internet to access his favorite video games.

Life before Internet

In the minds of the current generation, it is hard to imagine life without Internet. My 5 and a half-year old grandson Ryan and 4-year old granddaughter Sara can access free video games through the Internet and watch movies on DVD's when I drive them home from the caregiver. Students can carry out research on topics they are learning in schools and Universities. Professionals requiring up-to-date information on technical and business matters generally sign in to the Internet via lap top or desk top computers and can access information that is current even in terms of hours.

Life was quite different in the "olden days" (as my grandchildren call the time when my generation was their age). When I was 7 years old (just after World War II in rural Hungary) we saw a few cars, trucks were more frequent, and we travelled mainly on trains and buses when we had to go to the big city. Otherwise, we walked for hours, rode on horse drawn carriages, and the more affluent people got to places on bicycles. We listened to the commentary of soccer games at one of three radios that was available in the village of 800 people. The word television was unknown to us but we could watch a movie in the community centre on Saturday nights.

During University years (1960's) we did our research by going to libraries and looking up books and publications. Our essays contained information that was often 2 to 3 years old, especially when we quoted authors in published journals. We submitted these essays in hand-written form on hard-copy paper. A few students were able to use a typewriter which at times earned them a few extra points through the marking system.

During the early part of our professional careers (1970's and 1980's) we conducted our research work by reading books (which were published a few or more years earlier) and scientific journals. In order to project an image that our knowledge of the technology was "up-to-date" we generally quoted fellow scientists by stating that the information was obtained through "personal communications".

We witnessed some major breakthroughs in the 1970's with the word processing phenomenon. We threw away the carbon paper and connected the electric typewriters to magnetic tape machines so that we could make changes in the documents and re-print them. This made a major impact on the typing pool in large offices, often resulting in re-assignment of secretaries to other duties. The next phase in the modernization of office practices involved word processing technology with spell checking capabilities.

The most exciting development occurred in 1991 when World Wide Web was introduced by Tim Berners-Lee and Robert Cailau. In 1993 the first proper web-browser (Mosaic) gave a jump start to the Internet. Services were then set up for domain registration and sites began turning up on the web, running on basic HTML. Web had over 600% annual growth rate as important sites such as the White House and Pizza Hut appeared, followed by on-line shopping sites. In the mid 1990, Internet Service Providers (ISP's) such as AOL and CompuServe began offering Internet access to the masses.

Internet is now an integral part of our everyday lives. Many of us are not satisfied by accessing the Internet via desk-top and lap-top computers, we feel the need to be connected even when we are away from office or home. Smart phones such as BlackBerry are impacting our lives by providing wireless Internet access from almost anywhere so we can respond to important e-mails right away, as well as can track our travels with GPS and on-line digital maps.

I often think: how did we manage in the olden days without Internet?

Earth Day

Last week my grandchildren, Sara (Jr. Kindergarten) and Ryan (Sr. Kindergarten) came home from school and gave me a long talk about Mother Earth, telling me how important it is to look after it. They learned about Mother Earth in school in preparation for Earth Day; on April 22nd 2009 they have invited me to join them in school to celebrate Mother Earth. I was deeply moved by their genuine concern and understanding about the importance of protecting Mother Earth so that their generation will be able to enjoy the benefits of life around them. They talked about elephants, tigers, snakes, birds, and other "cool" animals, all needing Mother Earth to protect them. Ryan as an older brother then told his sister: "we need Mother Earth, too Sara".

Earth Day celebrations started in 1970 through the efforts of U.S. Senator Gaylord Nelson of Wisconsin, designed to inspire awareness and appreciation for the Earth's environment. Senator Nelson chose the date as the one that could maximize participation on college campuses for what he conceived as an environmental teach-in. He determined that the week of April 19-25 was the best bet because it did not fall during exams or spring breaks, did not conflict with religious holidays such as Easter or Passover, and was late enough in spring to have decent weather. Over 20 million people participated in 1970 and Earth Day is now observed each year on April 22 by more than 500 million people and national governments in 175 countries.

In the spirit of reflecting on Earth Day I watched a documentary called "An Inconvenient Truth" where former U.S. Vice President Al Gore passionately conveyed that humanity is sitting on a ticking time bomb. If the vast majority of the world's scientists are right, we have just ten years to avert a major catastrophe that could send our entire planet into a tail-spin of epic destruction involving extreme weather, floods, droughts, epidemics and killer heat waves beyond anything we have ever experienced. The film brilliantly portrays Gore's personal journey: from an idealistic college student who first saw a massive environmental crisis looming; to a young Senator facing a harrowing family tragedy that altered his perspective, to the man who almost became President of the United States but instead returned to the most important cause of his life - convinced that there is still time to make a difference. With wit, smarts and hope, the documentary brings home Gore's persuasive argument that we can no longer afford to view global warming as a political issue -

rather, it is the biggest moral challenge facing our global civilization.

After losing the Presidential race, Al Gore's vision was not well accepted by the Republican political circles and some of the industry. For example, the American auto industry colluded with the Bush administration in 2001 to scrap Al Gore's voluntary Partnership for a New Generation of Vehicles, which was on target to market fuel-efficient vehicles by 2003. With cheap oil and gas-guzzling SUVs dominating the market then, Bush and the auto industry thought there was little market for extremely fuel efficient vehicles. Instead of invading and occupying Iraq to secure long-term access to cheap oil, the U.S. would have been better off investing the over $600 billion spent on the war into environmentally friendly technology. But, as Gore states in the documentary, political will is a renewable resource. While the world would be a lot different if Americans elected Al Gore as president in 2000 instead of George W. Bush, the people made the necessary corrective action in 2008 by electing Barack Obama as President. In this new political climate, we all need to help the generations of Ryan and Sara in protecting Mother Earth!

About the Nobel Peace Prize

Former Finnish President Martti Ahtisaari won the Nobel Peace Price on Friday, October 10, 2008. The Norwegian Nobel Committee said it honoured Ahtisaari for important efforts over more than three decades to resolve international conflicts. The award includes a gift of $1.3 million.

The founder of the Peace Prize, Alfred Nobel was born on October 21, 1833 in Stockholm Sweden. His father was an engineer and inventor. In 1842, Nobel's family moved to St. Petersburg, Russia where his father had opened an engineering firm providing equipment for the Tsar's armies. In 1850, Nobel's father sent him abroad to study chemical engineering. During a two-year period Nobel visited Sweden, Germany, France and the United States. He returned to Sweden in 1863 where he devoted himself to the study of explosives. He was particularly interested in the safe manufacture and use of nitro-glycerine, a highly unstable explosive. Nobel incorporated nitro-glycerine into silica, an inert substance, which made it safer and easier to manipulate. This he patented in 1867 under the name of 'dynamite'. Dynamite established Nobel's fame and was soon used in blasting tunnels, cutting canals and building railways and roads all over the world. In the 1870s and 1880s, Nobel built up a network of factories all over Europe to manufacture explosives. He continued to work in his laboratory, inventing a number of synthetic materials and by the time of his death he had 355 patents. In November 1895, Nobel signed his will providing for the establishment of the Nobel Prizes. He set aside the bulk of his huge fortune to establish annual prizes in Physics, Chemistry, Physiology or Medicine, Literature and Peace. An Economics Prize was added later. Nobel died on December 10th 1896.

The Nobel Peace Prize was first awarded in 1901 to Frédéric Passy of France (Founder and President, Société d'arbitrage entre les Nations) and Henry Dunant of Switzerland (Founder of the International Committee of the Red Cross). High profile winners of the Nobel Peace Prize include:

- Theodore Roosevelt (1906), US President, for brokering the Treaty of Portsmouth ending the Russo-Japanese War;
- Woodrow Wilson (1919), US President, for being the foremost promoter of League of Nations;
- Albert Schweitzer (1952) for his philosophy of "Reverence for Life", expressed in many ways, but most famously in founding the Lambaréné Hospital in Gabon;

- Lester B. Pearson (1957) for introducing peacekeeping forces to resolve the Suez Crisis;
- Martin Luther King, Jr. (1964) for campaigning for civil rights;
- Mother Teresa (1979) for poverty awareness campaigning and service to humanity;
- Mikhail Gorbachev (1990) for his leading role in the peace process which today characterizes important parts of the international community;
- Jimmy Carter (2002), US President, for untiring effort to find peaceful solutions to international conflicts, to advance democracy and human rights, and to promote economic and social development; and
- Al Gore (2007) for efforts to build up and disseminate greater knowledge about man-made climate change, and to lay the foundations for the measures that are needed to counteract such change.

Nobel did not leave an explanation for choosing peace as a prize category. The categories for chemistry and physics were obvious choices as he was a trained chemical engineer. The reason behind the peace prize is less clear. He may have established it as a way to compensate for developing and manufacturing destructive forces. There is also some evidence that he was influenced by his former personal secretary, Bertha von Suttner, who worked for him for a short time in 1876 in Paris. Bertha von Suttner became a leading figure in the peace movement with the publication of her novel, *Die Waffen nieder!* (*Lay Down Your Arms!*) in 1889 and founded an Austrian pacifist organization in 1891. She was also editor of the international pacifist journal *Die Waffen nieder!*, from 1892 to 1899. Until Nobel's death, the two maintained regular contacts through correspondence. Hence it was fitting that she was the first woman to win the Nobel Peace Prize in 1005.

At the Genesis of Computer Age

I entered graduate school at the University of Toronto in September 1967, majoring in biometrics. I used a Facet mechanical calculator and a slide rule to do most of the required calculations. The most exciting phase of the year was when my class was offered a series of tutorials on computer science. We used IBM punch cards and IBM 360 series of computers, starting with model 20 which had 4K of core memory and eight 16 bit registers.

After graduating in 1969 I worked at the Great Lakes Forest Research Centre (GLFRC) in Sault Ste. Marie, Ontario. I had the exciting task of setting up statistical analysis software packages, such as regression and analysis of variance, on an IBM 1130 computer using Fortran compiler running on 4K words of core. The IBM 1130 was an efficient Fortran machine, I would load up in the evening a box (18 inches long) of IBM punch cards of data to derive a set of regression equations and the results would be ready by the next morning. Previously, it took us weeks to do a least squares fit with mechanical calculating machines.

In the early 1970's I worked as a research scientist with the Canadian Forestry Service, with focus on developing computer simulation models to mimic the growth of forest trees and stands. At that time we entered into an exciting new era, the advent of time sharing computer systems. I developed the Fortran version of the simulation model in an IBM CP/CMS environment, accessing the mainframe computer, located in Toronto, through telephone modem from Sault Ste. Marie. To access the main frame computer I used a terminal, consisting of an IBM selectric typewriter connected to a magnetic tape storage device and a telephone modem. I was now able to store my Fortran based simulation model on magnetic cards and upload it to the mainframe computer. In 1972 I got a call from Ian Sharp, President of I.P Sharp Associates, inviting me to visit him in Toronto. I.P Sharp Associates (IPSA) was a major Canadian computer time sharing, consulting and services firm of the 1970s and 80s. IPSA was particularly well known for its work on the APL programming language, developed by Ken Iverson. During my visit, Ian offered me a loan of his personal computer terminal and a free account on his mainframe system for 3 months in exchange that I translate my simulation model from Fortran to APL and publicize the advantages of APL. That state-of-the-art computer terminal used a dial-up acoustically coupled modem, operating at 300 baud, to access the main frame computer via telephone. It did not have a built in display, for that we used the regular television set.

In March 1973 it was time for me to come through with my commitment to Ian Sharp. GLFRC invited leading scientists from North America, including the editor of the Forest Science Journal, to witness a demonstration of my computer simulation model, first running in Fortran then switched over to APL environment. The demonstration took place in the auditorium of the local community college where television sets were suspended from the ceiling and wired into a central feed. We managed to connect the terminal into this feed so that the audience could see the interactive progress of the computer simulation model describing forest growth and development.

When I look back over 35 years, I am amazed at the progress that has been made in computer science. Our needs and expectations have also changed. I decided to share this bit of history with our readers (including myself) as a reality check when we complain about the speed of our laptops and internet access. I am currently using a Dell Latitude D830 laptop with 2 GB of memory and 120 GB of hard drive, supplemented with BlackBerry

Curve 8310 with built in GPS, integrated camera and quad band GPRS/EDGE network. I still wonder how I ever managed to get through the late 60's and early 70's with that ancient technology?

Book Publishing

It is the dream of most first time authors to be a best selling author. Yet the sobering statistics about the book industry provide a painful reality check that the probability of achieving that goal is very low.

It is estimated that about 1 million new books are published each year worldwide. United Kingdom appears to lead with over 200,000 new titles being released each year, followed by Unites States (172,000), China (136,000) and Germany (96,000); Canada is averaging close to 20,000 new books per year. While best selling authors count their numbers sold in millions, over 90% of the new titles end up selling less than 1,000 copies. A large percentage of new titles hit the market through the self publishing route and hence lack any sizeable distribution infrastructure. Printing companies who service self publishing authors are often reluctant to do business with the larger book stores mainly because when unsold books are returned to them they are forced to absorb the printing costs.

First time authors generally have few options available to them in the publishing industry. After finishing the manuscript, the next step is to write a brief synopsis which can then be used to find a publisher. Some authors opt to get a Literary Agent to represent them to publishers. There is no guarantee that this approach will work and it could cost about $500 or more. Publishing companies with established distribution network rarely take the work of first time authors, especially if the manuscript deals with autobiography. Consequently, the next logical step is to find a printing (small scale publishing) company and proceed with the self publishing option. At this point some authors chose to engage the services of an editor (at costs ranging from $500 to $1,000) to position the manuscript to be market ready. Next the printing company will supply a formatting specialist (at a cost of about $500) to prepare the manuscript to be print ready. Decision at this point can be costly. Some printing companies may advise the author to print 1,000 to 2,000 copies of their book right at the start in order to reduce the printing costs by approximately 50%. For an average book of 60,000 to 80,000 words the printing may still cost up to $5 per copy, hence requiring the author to invest $5,000 to $10,000. A self publishing author without a large scale distribution network is likely to sell about 500 books during the first two years. Many authors who have taken this route freely admit that they still have boxes of their book in the basement!

Another option for a first time author is to print initially 200 copies at a higher cost such as $10 each (investment is reduced to $2,000), then sell each book for $20 and recover the investment during the first year with a modest amount of profit. Following that, the printing costs of 100 copies each time can be covered from the profits of previous batches. This approach provides an efficient option for "testing" the market and if the sales start to increase then the author can start printing larges batches to reduce costs. I used this option with an Ottawa publishing company (Baico Publishing www.baico.ca) and have found it highly cost effective.

A relatively new phenomenon that is available to authors is to make the manuscript available as eBook through a company that is linked to major international book sellers. I explored this option with www.lightningsource.com and my first book "Dare to Take the Next Step – Adventures of a Refugee" is now included in the catalogues of several major eBook distribution companies (e.g. website: http://www.booksonboard.com/index.html Search: Hegyi). This option requires a relatively small amount of investment (less than $100), the eBook can then be purchased online for less than $10 and still yielding the author approximately $4 per book.

Futuristic Trends in Publishing

The publishing industry is rapidly changing from the traditional hard copy format to electronic books (eBooks) that can be downloaded wirelessly to hand-held computers at half the cost than those being sold in book stores. Bookstores as we know them now will gradually transform into digital outlets, selling eBooks and Print on Demand (POD) versions or simply go out of business.

This transition is being pushed on two critical fronts: "traditional" publishing companies who cater mainly to established authors will be forced to share the market place with visionary hi-tech competitors such as Lightning Source; and book stores stocked with hard copy products will gradually lose their market share to web-based companies such as Amazon.ca, e-books.com and diesel-ebook.com.

Lightning Source was formed in 1997 with the advent of print on demand technology. As a member of the Ingram family of companies, they draw from the strength, experience and global relationships of their parent company. They have taken the print on demand technology and refined it into a finely tuned print and distribution model which is revolutionizing the publishing business by uniting the world of publishers and consumers into an interactive community where even the most obscure titles can be accessed as easily as a current best-seller.

Publishing companies of any size can benefit from the Lightning Source POD model by eliminating the guess work in ordering, reducing the cost of warehousing, eliminating the need for keeping an inventory of books and pulping (print only what is needed). In addition, new titles can be uploaded as PDF files and made available to customers at half the cost of their POD counterpart through secure downloads. But the most significant benefit that the Lightning Source infrastructure offers is connectivity to a highly comprehensive distribution channel of book wholesalers and retailers at low cost and minimal risks. Using Ingram's distribution channel a new title always appears as in stock and available to over 30,000 wholesalers, retailers and booksellers in over 100 countries.

During the transition period, print on demand versions will dominate the marketplace. However, as readers get more familiar with a new breed of technology such as hand held computers optimized for eBooks, the momentum will shift from hard copy paper books to digital alternatives. Integrated hardware and software platforms are being introduced into the market place by several international companies. For example, Amazon.com released in November 2007 for the US market a software and hardware platform called Amazon Kindle for reading eBooks and other digital media. Three hardware devices, known as "Kindle", "Kindle 2," and "Kindle DX" support this platform, as does an iPhone application called "Kindle for iPhone. Hopefully, this technology will be available in the near future in Canada, too. Another technology that handles eBooks is BeBook which has been released recently into the market by a company from Holland (Endless Ideas BV). This technology facilitates reading any pdf*, mobi, lit*, epub*, html, txt, prc, fb2, jpg file and over 300,000 of free news feeds from BeBook, including Mobipocket Digital Rights Management support. BeBook offers unique paper-like display and long life battery (one charge will last 7.000 page turns).

In addition to the two devices listed above, over 20 such units have entered the market during the past 2 years. Further information on these devices is available at: http://en.wikipedia.org/wiki/List_of_e-book readers Pricing is between $300 and $500 but will be reduced as competitors move aggressively to control the market. The time has come that we can carry all the books we own in a small hand held device, as well as can download over 300,000 books for less than $10 each from anywhere with wireless connectivity.

Reduce Stress – Live Well

On June 4th I was an invited speaker at an international conference called GeoTec 2009 which was held in Vancouver, B.C. I was asked to talk about how Geographic Information Systems (GIS) was introduced 30 years ago into operational applications in forestry. I started my talk with some reminiscence that some 25 years ago as one of the pioneers of GIS applications, I used to make the circuit as invited keynote speaker at international conferences, talking about futuristic trends in the applications of GIS to natural resources management. How fast the years have passed: now in 2009 I have been invited to talk about the history of GIS. In the audience I recognized some friendly faces of former colleagues, looking a bit larger in size and with whiter hair (if any) than we all looked 25-30 years ago. But, the important thing was that we were glad to be there, still active in a profession that we loved over the years and still find the work exciting. One of the younger professionals asked me after the talk: "Are you ever going to retire?" I replied without any hesitation: "No, I am having too much fun keeping up with current trends, seeing that the dream we had in 1978 is a reality today due to the advances in technology". The next question was:

"How do you do it?" My answer to this question was: "With time and stress management".

Twenty eight years ago soon after I was appointed Director, Forest Inventory Branch, B.C. Forest Service, I was introduced to time management practices. This was orchestrated by my employer because my new job was expected to be highly stressful. I was to introduce computer assisted mapping into a highly traditional government department and basically replace manual draughting of maps with computer graphics technology.

Time management at that time was in hard copy format, using a 3-ring binder, each day had a page showing appointments, to do list and accomplished tasks. But the most important aspect of what I learned was that I had to set realistic goals and tasks for each day, record the results at the end of the day, reallocate those tasks which were not completed for another day to where there was an available window and remove any stress about what I had to do because now they were scheduled for action. This removed the stressful worry that used to dominate my days and the saying "I have so much to do I don't know where to start".

I still use time management as an important part of my daily activities. The hard copy format has been replaced by MS Outlook on my lap top computer and

BlackBerry, and the technical projects are being planned and monitored within the context of MS Project. I start each day around 6 am with reviewing accomplished tasks and setting new ones. I set my goals each day to complete all scheduled tasks by 4 pm then from 4:30 pm till 6 pm I schedule myself to look after my two grandchildren (Ryan 6½ and Sara 5 years old) and that period is the highlight of my day: I get some exercise and it keeps me feeling younger.

Besides time management, I minimize stress with having a sense of humour. With a small group of friends who enjoy situation-type of humour, I exchange tasteful jokes once or twice a week on the internet under the heading "smiles for the day". It is amazing how one or two minutes of humour can create a relaxed mindset during a busy day.

I have found that with a suitable time management practice, stress can be minimized and productivity can be improved. Scheduling activities should not stop with work related tasks; it can be extended to spending time with family and to recreational activities. Ultimately, this leads to a better quality of life and hopefully to a delayed expiry date.

Monitoring Natural Resources

Traditionally, Canada's natural resources have been mapped by labour- intensive methods that involve the following steps:

1. Vertical aerial photographs are acquired at various scales but mostly at 1:15,000

2. Skilled photo interpreters then view these photos with stereoscope and delineate the boundaries of homogeneous strata.

3. During spring and summer, field parties then visit the target area and obtain descriptions of a representative sample of forest and other resource types.

4. Following the field work, with the knowledge gained from ground sampling, aerial photo interpreters then assign a description to each stratum that includes species composition to the nearest 10%, age, tree height, crown closure and other relevant statistics.

The next step traditionally involved transferring the information from the aerial photographs to a paper map, followed by draughtsman neatly drawing the lines and descriptive statistics on mylar from which paper copies were made. In recent years, the introduction of new technology started to replace this process. In particular, the work of draughtsman has been modernized with computers and the information is entered directly into Geographic Information Systems (GIS). Some agencies have taken even a further step by replacing the hard copy based photo interpretation with a digital process, including viewing the digital imagery in stereo with software that facilitates both photo interpretation and the transfer of information directly into GIS.

Futuristic trends in the monitoring of Canada's natural resources are based largely on GIS technology. Spatial information is managed and retrieved in a rather sophisticated manner with state-of-the-art GIS software and depletions can be monitored cost effectively with satellite imagery. The next step in this development involves posting the GIS files on a web based platform, such as Google Earth and Virtual Earth. However, the most significant barrier in this development is in the business case currently offered by both Google and Microsoft. Forest companies and provincial/federal forest inventory department are reluctant to place their data that represents multi-million dollar investments on third party servers and then pay for accessing their own data.

Recent experiments with NASA's World Wind technology are showing promising results. GIS files, raster images and forest inventory samples can be accurately posted on a World Wind based platform and then the composite data can be accessed, analyzed and retrieved with plug-in software packages. There are developments currently ongoing in this area in an open-source software environment. Hence in the future resource managers will be able to sign in to a World Wind based platform which will function like Google Earth but with forest and multi resource inventory data. For example, queries such as find the location of forest stands allocated for harvesting, areas requiring planting or natural regeneration, forest stands damaged by fire or insects, forests containing commercially valuable species and areas that need to be protected for ecological reasons, can be made in a web based environment. In addition, digital forest cover maps can be evaluated in terms of their up-to-date status by comparing satellite imagery taken at the time the map was produced with a recent one and identifying the polygons that changed due to disturbances such as harvesting, fire, insects and diseases. After some ground checks on a representative sample, these polygons can then be updated on the GIS file; polygons that have not changed can be updated by projecting their attribute list over time with growth models. Implementation of such an approach will gradually phase out traditional re-inventory techniques and will lead to more cost effective continuous forest inventory practices and up-to-date GIS based forest cover maps. Besides accessing the web based platform with desk top and lap top computers, hand held computers equipped with GPS and wireless data transmission, such as iPod and BlackBerry, can be used in the field to access and update corporate data bases.

Golf is a good choice for Seniors

I didn't play any organized sport as I was growing up. In grade school we played some football (soccer), mostly just kicking the ball around without any rules or referees guiding us. In High School I was more interested in writing poetry than joining a football team, while in college I had to focus on studying because the working language (English) wasn't my mother tongue. My first exposure to organized sports was in the 70's working as a volunteer in minor hockey, supporting the teams of our two boys. In the 1980's as my weight gain started to be conspicuous, I realized that I needed to get involved in some activity so I started running. As my physical fitness improved, I joined a fitness club and started on nautilus weights, followed by aerobics.

Well, aerobics got my attention. I took part in one hour classes 3 times every week and on Saturdays I participated in the 90-minute super sweat high impact aerobic session. I was definitely hooked on aerobics and continued with the sport until it became rather conspicuous that I was out of the age group of most of the participants. But, fortunately at this time, I re-discovered golf when I was still in good shape to walk the 18 holes course. I was first introduced to golf in 1960 by my father-in-law in the country of this game's origin: Scotland. I was coached to play on a course in Edinburgh by a man who was in the top 10% of golfers which was good for me but visibly frustrating for my father-in-law. Since that time I played a few games each year, performing just marginally about the game of crocket. Then in 2001 I was on a business trip to India and some business associates invited me to join them for a game of golf at the prestigious Jaypee Greens in Noida. We played 18 holes, moved around in powered carts with helpful caddies; it was a very "civilized" way of playing the game, especially when afterwards we toasted our performance with a cold King Fisher beer in the air conditioned club house. So I was now hooked on golf and even taken some lessons to raise my skill set to 50 score on 9 holes courses Since the game at Jaypee Greens I have been playing golf regularly each year, mostly in Canada although I went back to India on business about 10 more times and managed to fit in a few games of golf during each trip.

For us seniors, some level of activity can be a life saver. Golf is a worthy candidate in this quest; if one still has the legs to move around, walking a 9 holes course in about two and a half hours is a good exercise. Otherwise, one can use a powered cart and can still get some workout through taking the shots at the ball. Once we master the game to some level of proficiency, watching PGA tours can be a lot of fun. Not meaning to offend team sports such as ice hockey, baseball, basketball or football, golf has some unique qualities as a game of professionals. Professional golfers are paid in direct proportion to how well they are playing. Golfers don't hold out for more money, demand new contracts or want to be traded because another player got a better deal. So, I enjoy watching the game on TV, as well as playing it for recreational purposes. I highly recommend golf for seniors as a fun vehicle to maintain a comfortable level of fitness.

Cancer Can be Beaten

About 30 years ago when a person was diagnosed with cancer, the reaction to it was like receiving a death sentence. There were three main reasons for this: early diagnosis was not a common practice, medical treatments for cancer were at their early stages and life style choices were at their infancy.

During the past 30 years, advances in medical research have changed the culture that when the word cancer is mentioned, we don't think of death sentence but we think of survival. I experienced this changing phenomenon. In 2004 I was diagnosed with prostate cancer. I was lucky because my cancer was detected at an early stage while doing the yearly physical examination. The oncologist recommended radiation as a suitable treatment. After the 37 sessions of radiation treatment, I was declared cancer free. However, cancer made me realize that I wanted to do so much more in my life. I got back to working full time and started writing a book with fellow cancer survivors Roslyn Franken, Jacquelin Holzman and Max Keeping as co-authors. We invited other cancer survivors to share their stories of survival; we received 32 incredible stories of courage and heart-warming experiences. We incorporated these stories in a book "Death Can Wait" and released it on August 23rd 2008 in Ottawa at the Dancing in the Street festivities of cancer survivors. All proceeds from the book are donated to support cancer research and the facilities to treat cancer patients.

A common element among cancer survivors is that we all made changes in our lifestyles to a healthier one and realized that every morning when we wake up is precious and time to celebrate. We also share the desire to help newly diagnosed cancer patients through support groups, one on one buddy system, raising money for cancer research, and by doing things that we always wanted but did not get around to do it (I call this after the famous movie "our bucket list").

An item on the bucket list of one of the contributors to Death Can Wait was playing in a band. Jennifer Baker began her journey on one fateful Friday the 13th in June, 2003 when she collapsed suddenly at work from a grand mal seizure. She was rushed to the hospital and 11 days later underwent brain surgery to remove a massive tumour from the right side of her brain. Pathology tests revealed her worst nightmare - a grade 3 Brain Cancer. She fought a courageous battle. Surgery and cancer treatments still left her with chronic headaches, insomnia, depression and even mild seizures. So she decided to take control of her life and sought help from a nutritionist who opened her eyes to enjoying good health the natural way. Five years later she was given a clean bill of health by her Oncologist. She has just started a new job as Director in an IT company, volunteers her time for a Brain Cancer Support Group, is working towards becoming a holistic nutritionist and plays drums in a band.

Each contributor to Death Can Wait has a unique story. We have dealt with this often life threatening disease in our way trusting the medical treatment chosen for us by the experts, keeping a positive attitude and making changes to live healthy lifestyles. Yes, we believe that Cancer can be beaten and consider each day as a day to celebrate life!

Stanley Cup Hockey

. On Friday, June 12th 2009 hockey fans were treated to one of the most exciting games in the history of ice hockey. At the Joe Louis Arena in Detroit, the highly favoured defending champions, the Detroit Red Wings, hosted the Pittsburgh Penguins for game 7 of the 2009 Stanley Cup championship. Just a year ago, the Red Wings defeated the Penguins by winning after 6 games the 7 game playoffs. Many hockey fans thought that history will repeat itself in 2009 as Detroit was ahead 4-3 after game 5. Game 6 was played in Pittsburgh on June 9th and the penguins defeated the Red Wings 2-1 in a game that could have gone either way right to the end. So as the two top teams in the National Hockey League (NHL) entered the final game, momentum was on Pittsburgh side. Penguins' player Max Talbot scored both goals, sending the Penguins to a 2-1 victory over the defending champions. Penguins' captain Sidney Crosby, who was injured near the end of the 2nd period, was still able to skate with the Stanley Cup as the youngest NHL captain (21 years old) to win this coveted championship. In the 2009 playoff championship, Crosby scored 15 goals and assisted in 16, a record that has set him on the road to becoming another hockey legend like Wayne Gretzky.

In Canada there are over half a million boys play minor hockey in different age categories. These age categories include pre-Novice (under 7 year old), Novice (8), Atom (9 and 10), Pee Wee (11 and 12), Bantam (13 and 14), and Midget (15-17). Many of these young hockey players pick one or two NHL players as their role model and those with a competitive nature, often dream of playing in the NHL when they grow up. Playing for the Stanley Cup is the ultimate "dream" far, far away from practical reality. There are thousands of men and women volunteering their time to help these young players, both boys and girls, learning the skill of the game along with sportsmanship, team spirit and social skills. As a former coach, team manager and Association President, I look back on the 10 years I spend in Minor Hockey as one of the most rewarding times in my life. I was coaching a Pee Wee team where my son Michael was the captain. Mike never made it to the NHL, but managed to play for a couple of years in Midget rep (touring team) and is still playing adult recreational hockey. He has also been coaching for many years, including being the Head Coach of a Minor Hockey Association in Waunakee, Wisconsin. My grandson Nathan also played minor hockey as well as became a level 3 referee. I had the pleasure of watching him referee a game with his Dad as a linesman!

On Friday night when I watched the NHL playoff championship, my thoughts drifted back to 1973 when I managed the Novice Tournament team in Sault Ste. Marie, ON with Walter Dubas (former Grey Hounds coach) as the head coach. The captain of the team was Ronnie Frances a 9 year old very talented player who set his dream at playing in the NHL. Ron Francis made it to the NHL in 1981 and played for Hartford Whalers for nearly 10 seasons, serving as Captain for 6. In 1991 he was traded to Pittsburgh Penguins where he played seven seasons and captaining two. Ron was a key player with the Penguins when they won their first Stanley Cup in 1990-91 season; he centered the formidable second line behind Mario Lemieux. The next season he led the team in the absence of Lemieux to another Stanley Cup, scoring the Cup-clinching goal against the Chicago Blackhawks.

Yes, dreams can come true, but for me, the most important part of working with young players was the opportunity of making a difference in their early development.

Impacts of NHL's Comedy of Errors

There was a time in my life that I was completely hooked on hockey. It started in 1970 when our two sons got enrolled in pee wee hockey in Sault Ste. Marie, Ontario. There was a shortage of adults to help out with the teams, so I volunteered first as a team manager, then a year later moved up to coaching. In 1973 I was asked to manage the Soo Novice Tournament team which was coached by Walter Dubas, a former coach of the Soo Greyhounds, an OHL Junior Hockey team. Our star player and team Captain was 9-year old Ronnie Frances who ended up having a successful career in the NHL, including leading his team to two Stanley Cup championships. When we moved to Victoria, B.C. in 1974 I got involved in hockey administration. I spent a year as President of the Oak Bay Minor Hockey Association and two years as President of the South Vancouver Minor Hockey Association. During the past 30 years I attended many NHL hockey games and without any question, hockey has been my favorite game.

However, recently I have been somewhat disillusioned with some of the developments in the NHL. It started in the 1998-99 season with the dispute between Alexei Yashin and the Ottawa Senators. In my opinion, this NHL super star lost perspective of the importance of delivering entertainment to the fans; he was also grossly overpaid, but still wanted more money. Then my disappointment escalated with the 2004-05 strike/lockout when the entire season was cancelled. During the lockout I became accustomed not to watch NHL hockey so when the labour dispute was settled, I was no longer interested in spending between $100 and $300 per game to attend live hockey games. Then this year the demands of Dany Heatley to be traded and the circumstances under which the negotiations progressed further confirmed my disillusionment with the NHL contract practices. It appears that there is a greater emphasis on the business interests of the "sport" than delivering entertainment to the fans.

Fortunately, a major turning point in my outlook occurred this past weekend. Sault Ste. Marie MP Tony Martin and former Soo resident Bob Diotte organized a reunion for the ex Saultite community on the occasion of the OHL Junior Hockey game between the Soo Greyhounds and the Ottawa 67's on September 27th 2009 at 2 pm in the Ottawa Civic Centre. As former residents of the Soo, my wife and I attended the game. Well, what a treat! We had excellent seats for a modest price ($16 each) and the hockey was exciting. It brought back memories of old times when I had the privilege of working with young players who skated their hearts out for the love of the game. Both the Soo Greyhound and Ottawa 67 players showed hockey skills often as good as we see in the NHL by the highly paid players. After the game the Soo Greyhound players dropped in to meet us ex Saultites and thanked us for coming out to their game. They were well dressed, polite and behaved in a way that gives praise to the many volunteers who worked with them as they moved up to this level of hockey.

The best seats in the Ottawa Civic Centre at OHL Junior Hockey are at a very modest price of $16. This season, my wife and I will be attending live hockey games at the OHL Junior Hockey level rather than at the NHL. On TV I will be watching most likely golf where the players are rewarded according to their production rather than through contract negotiations.

About Thanksgiving Day

In today's world, thanksgiving is when families get together for a feast to celebrate the year for a number of reasons such as abundant food, being free of sickness, surviving life threatening illness or just living in a peaceful environment without war or terrorist destructions.

The first recorded Thanksgiving ceremony took place on September 8, 1565, when 600 Spanish settlers, under the leadership of Pedro Menéndez de Avilés, landed at what is now St. Augustine, Florida. They held a Mass of Thanksgiving for their safe delivery to the New World; there followed a feast and celebration. The modern Thanksgiving holiday traces its origins from a 1621 celebration at the Plymouth Plantation, where the Plymouth settlers threw a harvest feast after a successful growing season. It is this iconic event that is generally referred to as the "First Thanksgiving." Thereafter, thanksgiving was celebrated on different days without an official proclamation. In the middle of the American Civil War, President Abraham Lincoln proclaimed a national Thanksgiving Day, to be celebrated on the final Thursday in November 1863.

In Canada, various First Nations had long-standing traditions celebrating the harvest and giving thanks for a successful bounty of crops. They organized harvest festivals, ceremonial dances, and other celebrations of thanks for centuries before the arrival of Europeans in North America. The European influence on Thanksgiving in Canada goes back to an explorer, Martin Frobisher, who had been trying to find a northern passage to the Pacific Ocean. Frobisher's Thanksgiving was not for harvest but for homecoming. He had safely returned from a search for the Northwest Passage. In the year 1578, he held a formal ceremony, in what is now the province of Newfoundland and Labrador, to give thanks for surviving the long journey. The feast was one of the first Thanksgiving celebrations by Europeans in North America. Starting in 1879 Thanksgiving Day was observed every year, but the date was set annually and changed year to year. In its early years it was for an abundant harvest and occasionally for a special anniversary.

After World War I, both Armistice Day and Thanksgiving were celebrated on the Monday of the week in which November 11 occurred. In 1931, the two days became separate holidays, and Armistice Day was renamed Remembrance Day. On January 31, 1957, the Canadian Parliament proclaimed: "A

Day of General Thanksgiving to Almighty God for the bountiful harvest with which Canada has been blessed ... to be observed on the 2nd Monday in October".

My family has always celebrated thanksgiving with a big feast, which includes turkey, ham, mashed potatoes with gravy, broccoli, cauliflower, carrots, Ukrainian cabbage rolls, different salads, and of course pumpkin pie with whipped cream. For the first time my wife (Rose) and I celebrated Thanksgiving by going on a trip: we drove to Orillia to visit our son and family. While the feast was pretty much the same, some of the other activities were unique. On Thursday night we were treated to a concert by Bobby Vinton and his musical band. It was a remarkable performance; the 74 year-old singer hasn't lost any of his magic and quality of singing. Then on Saturday night we went to another concert: the Oakridge Boys. This was also highly entertaining. Since both performances were at the Rama Casino, we went to try our luck both at the casino an hour before the shows. We have strict rules: $20 each maximum, when we lose it, it is for entertainment with no regrets. Rose succeeded in this mission in half an hour both times. Luck was with me this time, on Thursday night I won $7 and on Saturday night $200.

Well, there are many ways to celebrate Thanksgiving, but the most precious one is when we do it with family.

Community Spirit

The world is going through tough economic times. Greed and mismanagement by some corporate leaders, as well as the senseless war by the Bush administration has brought about losses of thousands of jobs and reductions in the values of life-time savings that were to help seniors during their retirement years. Yet this weekend, community spirit by Ottawa residents was at its best. On Sunday May 3rd 2009 over 5,000 cyclists, in-line skaters, walkers and corporate sponsors got together to raise money for kids with cancer at the Children's Hospital of Eastern Ontario (CHEO). For the past 11 years this event was known as the Nortel Tour and raised close to $ 5 million to help kids with cancer. Due to the economic crises of Nortel, this year this fund-raising event was marketed under a new name: CN Cycle for CHEO but it was still held at the Nortel Carling Campus where many of the Company's employees volunteered their time to make it a success. In addition, Nortel workers won the Ottawa Citizen Corporate Challenge by raising $45,180. In total, about $565,000 was raised by the community.

Last year was the first time I participated in this event. To celebrate my 70th birthday and recovery from prostate cancer, my grandson Ryan (5 years old at that time) and I participated in the 12 K bicycle ride and together we raised $750. We were ready to participate this year again but on April 15th I had a bad fall on the stairs and ended up with a few cracked ribs, unable to ride the bike. Ryan still wanted to ride and talked his Dad into riding with him. Ryan put me in charge of fund raising, although he still went door to door in our neighbourhood asking for pledges. He was so proud as he was approaching the finish line with his Dad who is battling brain cancer. His goal was to raise $800.00 (to beat our combined record of last year) and he succeeded by exceeding $900.00.

It was heart warming to see so many families participating in CN Cycle for CHEO. Children of various ages riding with their Mum and Dad, sporting a wide range of cycling outfits and showing the registration number on the back of their T-shirt (each registrant got a T-shirt if they raised $75 or more). The event clearly showed that residents of Ottawa came together in a community spirit to help kids with cancer. Many of us had tears in out eyes when MC Max Keeping introduced the 2009 MacDonald's Dream Team members Isla MacIntosh (5), Evan Simms (9) and Sean Leslie (16) who represented the children and youth who rely on CHEO to help them in their journey of recovering from cancer. Isla announced that her cancer was in remission and gave everyone a big smile. Evan drew a smile from all in attendance when he said that he was proud as he crossed the finish line. Sean was beaming as he announced that the treatments have been successful and he is ready to get back to show jumping with his horse.

We are indeed lucky in Ottawa that we have such excellent facilities to treat cancer, especially when the little ones are affected, and that the residents of Ottawa come out in full force to help with the fundraising required to support these facilities.

Message to Grandparents re Facebook

If you are a Grandma of Grandpa and over 65, you probably see your grandchildren 2 or 3 times a year. The chances are that on these visits you don't get to know them really well, they may even treat you with a behaviour that you expect them to be rather than who they really are on a day to day basis. I got this idea when I read an article recently written by Beth DeFalco of Associate Press (March 12, 2009) on "Grandparents, grandchildren interact on Facebook", saying that "when your 88-year-old grandfather sends a request to be your friend on Facebook, you have two choices: either confirm it, then quickly take down all those party pictures you thought were so funny, or plan on never coming home for the holidays".

Facebook is a free-access social networking website that is operated by Facebook, Inc. Users can join networks and can add friends and send them messages, and update their personal profiles to notify friends about themselves. Facebook came about as a spin-off of a Harvard University version of Hot or Not. Mark Zuckerberg, while attending Harvard as a sophomore, founded "The Facebook" on February 4, 2004. It quickly became a success at Harvard and more than two-thirds of the school's students signed up in the first two weeks. It started off as just a "Harvard-Thing," until Zuckerberg decided to spread Facebook to other schools and enlisted the help of roommate Dustin Moskovitz. They first spread it to Stanford, Dartmouth, Columbia, Cornell and Yale, and then to other schools with social contacts with Harvard. Now Facebook is operated through Facebook Inc. with Zuckerberg as its CEO. On October 24, 2007, Facebook Inc. sold a 1.6% stake to Microsoft Corp. for $240 million, spurning a competing offer from online search leader Google Inc. This would indicate that Facebook had a market value of $15 billion at the time of the sale.

So, Grandparents, signing up on Facebook looks like a safe bet, it is no longer just for college students and the company is likely to be around some time. Currently, there are over 175 million users of Facebook, more than half are outside of college, and an average user has 120 friends on the site. More than 28 million pieces of content (web links, news stories, blog posts, notes, photos, etc.) shared and over 850 million photos uploaded to the site each month.

If you want to get signed up on Facebook, you can find detailed instructions on http://www.wikihow.com/Create-a-Facebook-Profile.

After registering, you will have to go through a series of steps to personalize your profile. First, face book will offer to scour your email address book for people who are on face book and whom you can invite to be your friends. Simply enter your email address and password, and face book will find your friends. Select the ones you want to add by ticking the boxes to the left of their pictures, and then click 'add to friends' at the bottom. Also you'll be able to choose friends from your email address book who aren't on face book and send an email to them inviting them to join up and be your friend.

But, don't use Facebook as a tool to spy on your grandchildren, but as a medium to connect with them. They will be proud of you for being "cool" and keeping connected with their network of communications. They will be proud to share your pictures with their friends. I am proud that my daughter posted a picture of me with two of the grandchildren on her Facebook. Get connected!

Remembrance Day

Every year, on 11 November at 11 am – the eleventh hour of the eleventh day of the eleventh month – we pause to remember those men and women who have died or suffered in all wars, conflicts and peace operations since the beginning of the 20th century.

I remember the end of Second World War when as a young boy I lived with my parents in western Hungary. Near the end of the war, our village was occupied by German soldiers. I still remember the SS marching through the main street while we were hiding behind the window. The soldiers came into our house and my father was taken away by them, along with other men, to dig trenches as the front was retreating from Russia through Hungary. We did not see my father for a month, then one night he came home, managed to escape as the shooting escalated between the German and Russian soldiers. He told us that the front is expected to reach our village at any time and we had to prepare for it. The next morning my father, grandfather and mother started to dig in the backyard, making a bunker for us to hide in. It was a hole in the ground, about 8 feet by 8 feet by 8 feet, with about 2 feet of hay on the floor. At one end, they made steps so we could go into it, then placed wooden planks on top, covered it with soil from the garden to make it look like a large flower bed. The entrance was covered with hay so nobody would suspect that it was a bunker. Well, the fighting reached our village by evening, so my parents, grandfather and I took food and warm blankets with us to the bunker. At night we heard solders running outside, shouting in German, then in Russian. The fighting lasted for over a week as our village changed hands several times. When the fighting appeared to have stopped, my father took me back to the house to get more supplies. My grandfather stayed with my mother in the bunker to protect her in case some of the soldier would find our hiding place. As my father and I were returning from the house, the shooting started again, soldiers were chasing each other, as well as a low flying plane was spraying machine gun bullets to the side of our house. My father picked me up and run with me as bullets were hitting the ground and miraculously we made it back to the bunker without even an injury. We survived the war! But thousands of young men and women made the ultimate sacrifice for future generations.

Those of us who immigrated to Canada have been offered new opportunities because of the sacrifices made by Canadian men and women in wars as well as in peace keeping missions. So, on November 11th we honour those who fought for Canada in the First World War (1914-1918), the Second World War (1939-1945), and the Korean War (1950-1953), as well as those who have served since then. More than 1,500,000 Canadians have served their country in this way, and more than 100,000 have died. They gave their lives and their futures so that we may live in peace.

A symbol of remembrance in Canada and in many parts of the world is the red poppy. The poppy's significance to Remembrance Day is a result of Canadian military physician John McCrae's poem *In Flanders Fields*.

In Flanders fields the poppies blow
Between the crosses, row on row,
That mark our place; and in the sky
The larks, still bravely singing, fly
Scarce heard amid the guns below.

We are the dead. Short days ago
We lived, felt dawn, saw sunset glow,
Loved, and were loved, and now we lie
In Flanders fields.

Take up our quarrel with the foe:
To you from failing hands we throw

The torch; be yours to hold it high.
If ye break faith with us who die
We shall not sleep, though poppies grow
In Flanders fields.

The poppy emblem was chosen because of the poppies that bloomed across some of the worst battlefields of Flanders in World War I, their red colour an appropriate symbol for the bloodshed of trench warfare. A Frenchwoman, Anna E. Guérin, introduced the widely used artificial poppies given out today. (http://en.wikipedia.org/wiki/Remembrance_Day#Poppies).

Dancing in the Street

On August 23, 2008 from noon to 10 pm in Ottawa thousands came to dance on the street. Bank Street, between Glebe and Fifth Avenue, was closed and cancer survivors celebrated life with Honorary chair of "Dancing in the Street", Max Keeping, CTV Ottawa anchor. Max is a proud cancer survivor and promotes cancer awareness: "We need to change the culture, so that when the word is mentioned, we don't think death ...we think survival. Those of us who have been successful in fighting it need to share that with the world; we need to spotlight the amazing work researchers are doing to treat - and sometimes cure - the many cancers".

Cancer has afflicted humans throughout recorded history. The oldest description of cancer was discovered in Egypt and dates back to approximately 1600 B.C. The origin of the word *cancer* is credited to the Greek physician Hippocrates (460-370 B.C.). He used the terms *carcinos* and *carcinoma* to describe non-ulcer forming and ulcer-forming tumours. In Greek these words refer to a crab, most likely applied to the disease because the finger-like spreading projections from a cancer called to mind the shape of a crab. Treatments for cancer went through a slow

213

process of development. The ancients recognized that there was no curative treatment once a cancer had spread and that intervention might be more harmful than no treatment at all. Surgery then was very primitive with many complications, including blood loss. It wasn't until the 19th and early 20th centuries that major advances were made in general surgery and specifically in cancer surgery. In 1896 a German physics professor, Wilhelm Conrad Roentgen, discovered "X-ray", with "X" being the algebraic symbol for an unknown quantity. There was immediate worldwide excitement. Within months, systems were being devised to use X-rays for diagnosis, and within 3 years radiation was used in the treatment of cancer. Radiation therapy began with radium and with relatively low-voltage diagnostic machines. In France a major breakthrough took place when it was discovered that daily doses of radiation over several weeks would greatly improve therapeutic response. The methods and the machines for delivery of radiation therapy have steadily improved. Today, radiation is delivered with great precision in order to destroy malignant tumours while minimizing damage to adjacent normal tissue.

Over the years, the development and use of chemotherapy drugs have resulted in the successful treatment of many people with cancer. By the middle of the 20th century, scientists had in their hands the instruments needed to begin solving the complex problems of chemistry and biology presented by cancer. Scientists have learned more about cancer in the last decade of the 20th century than has been learned in all the centuries preceding.

In our modern times, cancer treatment is well structured and strongly focused on success. The web site of Canadian Cancer Society provides an excellent overview of the facilities available to treat cancer:

http://www.cancer.ca/Canada-wide/About%20cancer.aspx?sc_lang=en

Early diagnosis, effective medical treatments, diets and healthy life style are all important elements for surviving cancer. In addition, positive attitude at the time of diagnosis and during treatments is also an important element of survival.

Celebrating Canada Day

On July 1, 2009 Canadians celebrated their country's 142nd birthday.

Canada Day marks the creation of the Dominion of Canada in 1867. From its earliest settlements by Native Americans, through French and English settlements, Canada was a divided land. Some territories had banded together before 1867, but Confederation was the first large step toward total unity. On July 1, 1867 four North America Provinces (Nova Scotia, New Brunswick, Ontario and Quebec) formed a union in a federation under the name of Canada. On 20th June 1868, then Governor General Lord Monck issued a royal proclamation asking for Canadians to "celebrate the anniversary of the confederation." However, the holiday was not established statutorily until 1879, when it was designated as Dominion Day, in reference to the designation of the country as a Dominion in the British North America Act. The holiday was initially not dominant in the national calendar because Canadians thought of themselves as primarily British, and hence being less interested in celebrating distinctly Canadian forms of patriotism. No official celebrations were therefore held until 1917 – the 50th anniversary of Confederation – and then none again for a further decade (http://en.wikipedia.org/wiki/Canada_Day). Since 1958, the government has arranged for an annual observance of Canada's national day. The format provided for a Trooping the Colours ceremony on the lawn of Parliament Hill in the afternoon, a sunset ceremony in the evening followed by a mass band concert and fireworks display. On October 27, 1982, July 1st which was known as "Dominion Day" became "Canada Day". Since 1985, Canada Day Committees are established in each province and territory to plan, organize and coordinate the Canada Day celebrations locally. Currently, most communities across the country host organized celebrations for Canada Day, usually outdoor public events, such as parades, carnivals, festivals, barbecues, air and maritime shows, fireworks, and free musical concerts, as well as citizenship ceremonies for new citizens. The celebrations in the Capital are usually held on Parliament Hill, consisting of singing of O Canada, speeches by the Governor General, Prime Minister and other dignitaries, followed by entertainment. Thousands of Canadians take part in these celebrations, wearing red shirts and white pants/ skirts or simply wrapped in the maple leaf flag.

This year I was privileged to take part in a highly rewarding and warm Canada Day Celebrations. It was not on Parliament Hill like in previous years, but at the Aberdeen Pavilion, Lansdowne Park where over 3,000 seniors were treated with breakfast as part of the Mayor's Annual Canada Day Celebrations for Seniors. Although I could have qualified to be one of the invitees, I joined members of my service club (Ottawa Kiwanis club) to be one of the volunteers in serving the food. The Kiwanians were teamed up with volunteers of the Aga Khan Foundation and we had fun! As we served scrambled eggs, sausages, hash brown, croissant, and other "healthy goodies", we greeted the seniors with "Happy Canada Day" which always yielded a big smile and a response "Happy Canada Day to you, too". Ladies from the Aga Khan Foundation led the way in the exchange of greetings with smiles that penetrated the heart of many of our guests. T-shirts displaying "Proud to be Canadian" created "I am proud to be a new Canadian" response from many of us serving the food and a strong feeling of patriotism. I have often heard the comment that Canadians do not show their feelings of patriotism as much as our American neighbours do; well, we went all out on this Canada Day, busting in pride for being Canadians. Uniting in service is a very efficient way of bringing different cultures together and cultivating mutual respect for one another, the Canadian way!

Celebrating Father's Day

This year, June 21st 2009 was the first day of summer but more importantly, this day was also father's day. I seem to enjoy father's day more and more every year, being thankful to have a family and the health to celebrate it with. I still visited with my own father in thoughts and spirit even though he passed away 15 years ago. It was still nice to think back of the many quality times we were able to spend together. Although I was forced to leave my native land (Hungary) when I was 18 years old and we were not able to see each other over 17 years, we managed to make a few visits after the political situation eased a bit in the 1970's and 1980's. During those visits we re-connected and made up for lost time caused by the politics of the time. Because of this experience, I am especially grateful that in our democratic society, families can celebrate fathers' day without the obstacles imposed upon them by misguided political forces.

The history of Father's Day dates back to 1909 to Spokane, Washington (http://festivals.iloveindia.com/fathers-day/fathers-day-origin.html). Sonora Smart Dodd was listening to a Mother's Day sermon at the Central Methodist

Episcopal Church and was inspired to have a special day dedicated to her father, William Jackson Smart, who had brought her up single-handedly after her mother died. Sonora wanted to let her father know how deeply she was touched by his sacrifices, courage, selflessness and love. To pay a tribute to her dad, Sonora held the first Father's Day celebration on 19th of June 1910, on the birthday of her father. She was the first to solicit the idea of having an official Father's Day observance. However, unlike Mother's Day, which was readily accepted, Father's Day at that time was received with mockery and hilarity. But three years later a bill to make the day official was introduced and the idea was approved only three years later by US President Woodrow Wilson. In 1924, the idea of designating a day to honour fathers gained further momentum as it was supported by President Calvin Coolidge. In 1926, a National Father's Day Committee was formed in New York City. However, it was thirty years later that a Joint Resolution of Congress gave recognition to Father's Day. Another 16 years passed before President Richard Nixon in 1972 established the third Sunday of June, as a permanent national observance day of Father's Day. Today, over 52 countries have accepted the third Sunday in June to celebrate Father's day while other countries chose different dates to hour fathers.

While Father's Day celebrations take different forms, a common denominator is that sons and daughters express gratitude to their fathers for being there for them. This year I had one of the best Father's Day. My son Mike (who lives in the US) sent an e-Card that he designed, included in it was a picture of him, my daughter-in-law Penny, my grandson Nathan and my granddaughter Tassia; the message read: "Dad, thank you for being there for me". Then my daughter Jennifer, her husband Gil, grandson Ryan and granddaughter Sara took me to the Dragon Boat Festival in Ottawa where we had lunch and spent the rest of the afternoon watching the races and being entertained by some great musicians. It was truly a family affair and I especially enjoyed watching the grandchildren having a lot of fun. The day culminated by getting a framed picture of Ryan and Sara with a message: "Love you Papa".

As I am getting on in years, I value both Father's Day and Mother's Day more and more as a Family Day! These two days I especially recognize that for me, having children and grandchildren is the most important gift that life treated me with. Added to that is a very treasured gift for which I am especially grateful: both my son and daughter turned out to be very devoted parents. So this year I renamed Father's Day as Father's/Grandfather's Day!

International Women's Day

International Women's Day has been observed since in the early 1900's, a time of great expansion and turbulence in the industrialized world. Women's oppression and inequality was urging women to become more vocal and active in campaigning for change. In 1908, 15,000 women marched through New York City demanding shorter hours, better pay and voting rights. In 1909 in accordance with a declaration by the Socialist Party of America, the first National Woman's Day was observed across the United States on February 28th. In 1910 during the International Conference of Working Women Clara Zetkin, leader of the 'Women's Office' for the Social Democratic Party in Germany, came up with the idea of an International Women's Day. She proposed that every year in every country there should be a celebration on the same day - a Women's Day - to press for the demands of women. The conference of over 100 women from 17 countries, representing unions, socialist parties, working women's clubs, and including the first three women elected to the Finnish parliament, greeted Zetkin's suggestion with unanimous approval and thus International Women's Day was created.

Following the Copenhagen decision, International Women's Day (IWD) was honoured the first time in Austria, Denmark, Germany and Switzerland on March 19th. More than one million women and men attended IWD rallies campaigning for women's rights to work, vote, be trained, to hold public office and end discrimination. In 1913 Russian women observed their first International Women's Day on the last Sunday in February. In 1913 International Women's Day was transferred to 8 March and this day has remained the global date for International Women's Day ever since.

The new millennium has witnessed a significant change and attitudinal shift in both women's and society's thoughts about women's equality and emancipation. With more women in the boardroom, greater equality in legislative rights, and an increased critical mass of women's visibility as impressive role models in every aspect of life, one could think that women have gained true equality. However, the fact is that in many areas women are still not paid equally to that of their male counterparts, women still are not present in equal numbers in business or politics, and globally women's education, health and the violence against them is worse than that of men (for more information on this topic, see:
http://www.internationalwomensday.com/about.asp

In all, great improvements have been made since the early 1900's. Now, there are female astronauts, prime ministers, heads of states, CEO's of corporations, and women can work and have a family. And so the tone and nature of IWD has, for the past few years, moved to a certain extent from being a reminder about the negatives to a celebration of the positives.

While the world is celebrating the achievements of women, we cannot ignore some controversial status quo that still require major changes in mind set. For example, in Italy, Pope Benedict XVI told a Vatican crowd that he had been reflecting on the condition of women and praying that they can live with respect and dignity. Hearing this as a Roman Catholic I pray that the leadership of my church (including the Pope) be enlightened to realize that women have equal rights to men, including being ordained as priests! This same message is also applicable to other religious organizations where even the education of women is actively suppressed by men.

The Mystery of Halloween

Halloween is celebrated each year on October 31st. For many people, it represents a tradition when houses are decorated with some symbols of ghosts, spooky creatures, and of course the inside of pumpkins carved out and replaced by burning candles that glow in the dark outside the front steps or windows. Then to complete this picture of a traditional Halloween night, as soon as it gets dark, children dressed up in scary costumes go to houses and say "trick or treat" and open their bags to receive the "treats" of candies, chocolate bars and other small presents.

Halloween is one of the oldest and most popular holidays. Millions of people celebrate Halloween without knowing its origins and myths. It was originally a pagan holiday and dates back to over 2000 years ago. Halloween tradition can be traced back to the Celtic culture in Ireland, Britain and Northern Europe. Roots lay in the feast of Samhain, which was annually on October 31st to honour the dead. Samhain signifies "summers end" and was originally a harvest festival with sacred bonfires, marking the end of the Celtic year and beginning of a new one. Many of the practices involved in this celebration were fed on

229

superstition. The Celts believed the souls of the dead roamed the streets at night. Since not all spirits were thought to be friendly, gifts and treats were left out to pacify the evil and ensure next year's crops would be plentiful. This custom evolved into trick-or-treating.

When Christianity spread to parts of Europe, instead of trying to abolish these popular pagan customs, people tried to introduce ideas which reflected a more Christian view. Hence, Halloween has become a confusing mixture of traditions and practices from pagan cultures to Christianity. Then in the 7th century, Pope Boniface IV introduced All Saints' Day to honor saints and martyrs, basically to replace the pagan festival of the dead. Initially it was observed on May 13th but in 834, Gregory III moved All Saint's Day to November 1st and for Christians, this became an opportunity for remembering before God all the saints who had died and all the dead in the Christian community. October 31st thus became All Hallows' Eve ('hallow' means 'saint'). Numerous folk customs connected with the pagan observances for the dead have survived to the present.

Originally the Irish would carve out turnips or beets as lanterns as representations of the souls of the dead. In 1848, millions of Irish emigrants poured into America as a result of the potato famine and brought the tradition with them. However, they could not find many turnips to carve into lanterns but they did find an abundance of pumpkins. Pumpkins seemed to be a suitable substitute for the turnips and pumpkins have since been an essential part of Halloween celebrations.

Over the years, children have created their own versions of Halloween traditions. They look forward to dressing up in creative costumes, painting their faces to look scary, and filling the "loot" bags with all sorts of goodies. For us parents and grandparents, the main focus in these times must be safety for the children without spoiling the fun. In this respect, the activity that one of my daughter's friend is organizing appears to be the most appropriate one. Several school mates of her son and daughter (including our grandchildren) are invited with their parents to her house on October 31st for a pizza party. After the tummies are full, they all go out in the neighborhood to "trick or treat" under the watchful eyes of the parents. At the end of the evening the parents will be able to check out the goodies to ensure that they do not contain any harmful objects.

It is shaping up to be a truly fun Halloween night. I plan to help with the quality control of the goodies!

My Grandson is a Journalist

On Saturday, May 16th 2009 I attended the graduation ceremony at the School of Journalism in Missoula, Montana. It was most impressive as graduates and Professors talked about the challenges facing new graduates. It was a very proud occasion for me because my grandson Nat Hegyi was one of the graduates. What a proud moment it was when he received his degree. It was 48 years ago that I was wearing the black gown and hat when I graduated with a science degree. I was full of hope when I entered a new era in my professional career. Now, it was my grandson's turn.

As I was looking at the faces of the new graduates, my mind started to wonder what will they think when they reach the end of their journey? How will they be facing the challenges in a profession that is expected to play a key role in the shaping of the future of the next generation during these harsh economic times? Will they be able to report the truth without being used by special interest groups to promote an agenda that does not necessarily serve the interest of the population at large? Will they become infatuated with left wing ideas or trade in their ideals for economic gains and align themselves with the right wing? Or will they be able to serve their audience in an unbiased manner by reporting the truth in a realistic perspective?

Before going to the graduation ceremonies, I was watching TV in my hotel room. There were two programs that caught my attention. The first one involved a reporter interviewing a Roman Catholic Cardinal from Nigeria. It was a perfect interview from the Cardinal's point of view. The interviewer expressed her admiration for the good work and ultra conservative views of the Cardinal, what a great honour it was for her to be granted an interview by a priest who moved up to one of the highest ranks in the church. All the questions were presented as a great lead to promote the status quo in the church. There were no questions about the church's position on why women are denied opportunity to enter the priesthood. Abuses of young children by priest was conspicuously ignored and the Cardinal tried to leave the impression that there are no shortages of priests, in fact in some countries such as Nigeria, the church had absolutely no problem recruiting priests. The interviewer missed an opportunity of quoting well known statistics that show the complete opposite of what the Cardinal was stating. Hence viewers who are not aware of the truth were misled by this biased reporting. O course, the Cardinal was beaming...and the interviewer will get another interview at any time.

After all, such great publicity, free of charge, is priceless for the church but will it serve the interest of those Catholics who want changes in their beloved church?

The second interviewer, on the other hand, used more the approach that I hope the new graduates will adopt. The interview dealt with the controversy that the pro-life groups are promoting around the visit of President Barack Obama to the University of Notre Dame. The interviewer covered this delicate topic with skill and diplomacy, presenting the position of both sides in an unbiased manner. The extremist views were put in realistic perspectives with regard to the numbers they represented within the context of the entire population. The interviewer did his homework and provided information for his viewers that was informative and truthfully reported the current situation.

I was impressed with the speeches the representatives of the new graduates delivered during the graduation ceremony. They gave the impression that they were taught well about responsible reporting, they showed dedication to their chosen profession and are aware of the immense responsibility and challenges they are facing as they enter their professional life. More than ever in our history responsible reporting is needed as we are trying to recover from tough economic times and the terrorist attacks.

How I became a Kiwanian

In March 1972 I was coaching a Pee Wee hockey team in Sault Ste. Marie, Ontario which was sponsored by the Lakeshore Kiwanis Club. We won both the League and Playoff championships. As I was getting a treat for the boys I saw the sponsor of the team we just defeated was getting pop for the boys. That team was coached by Conrad (Con) Lauber. Jokingly I said to Con: "do you know anything about the Lakeshore Kiwanis club? We just won the playoff championship and they don't even buy pop for the boys". Con laughed and said: "your team, including their parents, will be treated to a banquet next Saturday". I said: "how do you know that?" He replied: "because I am President of the Lakeshore Kiwanis Club".

This was my first encounter with the Kiwanis organization. Con invited me to three meetings and following that he sponsored me to join the club. This was a very positive step in my life as I was trying to integrate into the Canadian way of life. When moved from Sault Ste. Marie to Victoria, B.C. in 1974, I transferred my membership to a club there and was welcomed warmly by my new Kiwanis friends who helped us to settle in our new environment. After chairing committees I was elected Club president in 1981-82. The challenge was to increase membership from 15 to 44 and with the stronger club we were able to build a service club at a High School, as well as one at the University of Victoria. Following that I became Lt. Governor of a Division in 1984-85 and Governor of the Pacific North West District in 1990-91. My wife Rose and I became so much richer by gaining many friends in the Kiwanis family and experiencing the joys of helping people in need. I have learned a lot about leadership, gained confidence in public speaking and most of all, became richer with the feeling that there are so many caring people in this world. Working with students at High School and University level, I was reassured that our future is in good hands as a new generation of caring young men and women are moving up to the task of leadership around the world.

Kiwanis International is a worldwide service organization. It focuses on the needs of ordinary people and children to create extraordinary life-changing moments. Kiwanis and its Service Leadership Programs boast a membership of more than 600,000 men, women, and youth in nearly 16,000 clubs in more than 70 countries and geographic areas. Members of Kiwanis and its Service Leadership Programs volunteer more than 21 million hours and invest more than $113 million in their communities around the world. Kiwanis International is the only service organization that builds leaders at every level: from the youngest Kiwanis Kids all the way through several youth programs and adult programs. Kiwanis' impact on the world will be measured by the 10 million young leaders it nurtures. Kiwanis continues its service emphasis of "Young Children: Priority One," which focuses on the special needs of children from prenatal development to age 5. I was privileged to sit on the international board when this program was introduced in 1990. In a typical year, "Young Children: Priority One" service projects involve more than US$14 million and 1 million volunteer hours. In 1994, Kiwanis launched its first Worldwide Service Project, a $75 million campaign in partnership with UNICEF to eliminate iodine deficiency disorders by the year 2000. IDD projects have been funded in 95 nations. Kiwanis International Foundation has raised nearly $100 million to eliminate IDD worldwide.

Yes, I feel good that 37 years ago I joined Kiwanis. I strongly recommend to new Canadians to join a service club and enjoy the many benefits that may come with such a venture.

The Day I met Lancelot Hogben

Professor Lancelot Hogben was invited in 1963 by Dr. Cheddi Jagan, Prime Minister of British Guiana, to help establish the University of British Guiana (now Guyana). As the University's first Vice Chancellor and Principal, he focused on assembling strong faculties in Arts, Natural Sciences and Social Sciences, as well as on fund raising and building facilities. Dr. Jagan also asked Prof. Hogben to head a "think tank" with the mandate of providing advice on social issues. Both Dr. Jagan and Prof. Hogben were left-leaning in their political convictions and members of the think tank were mostly self proclaimed socialists. A senior member of this group was Dr. Morrison Sharp, head of the University's History Faculty, who lost his job in the US during the era of McCarthyism. Dr. Sharp and I were neighbours and we often got together for a discussion on politics. In those days I was a strong anti-communist (former freedom fighter in the 1956 Hungarian revolution) and our discussions were quite lively. Dr. Sharp recommended to Prof. Hogben that I be invited to join the think tank, mainly to give a bit of balance to the discussions.

241

Meeting Prof. Hogben made a major impact on my life's journey. He was a brilliant man, knowledgeable in most areas of science, and members of the group referred to him as scientific humanist. During the first meeting I was asked to talk about what went wrong with socialism in Hungary. I argued that socialism was not given a chance to succeed because the communists turned against the people who brought them into power, i.e., the proletariat, the working class segment of the population. Communism was largely based on Marxism which, in my opinion, was incompatible with human nature. People who worked hard expected to get rewarded more than those who did not want to work. Prof. Hogben found Marxist dogma, dished out as dialectical materialism, deeply distasteful and wholly incompatible with his own criteria for intellectual integrity (as explained further in his autobiography published by his son Adrian). Listening to Prof. Hogben "lecture" to the think tank influenced my political views to be positioned somewhat in the middle. In addition, I was getting interested in his views on statistical theories and the popularisation of science in such a way as it was easy to understand.

After spending 3 years in British Guiana, I immigrated to Canada and enrolled in a M.Sc. program at the University of Toronto, majoring in

Biometrics with a minor in biological statistics. I was largely influenced in the selection of topics for my post graduate studies by Prof. Hogben. As my luck went, the professor of statistics was a student of R.A. Fisher who was a contemporary of Prof. Hogben and at times the two famous scientists disagreed on statistical methodology.

Prof. Hogben was an English zoologist and geneticist who wrote the best-selling book: *Mathematics for the Millions* (1933). He applied mathematical principles to genetics and was concerned with the way statistical methods were used in the biological and behavioural sciences. He held various academic posts in the UK, Canada, South Africa and British Guiana. During World War II he was put in charge of the medical statistics records for the British army. After the war he became professor of medical statistics at the University of Birmingham. A most interesting and comprehensive review of his career and scientific contributions can be found in an article written by Sahotra Sarkar in 1996 (see: http://www.genetics.org/cgi/reprint/142/3/655)

Importance of Local TV

Thousands of Ottawa residents turned out on Saturday, May 23rd 2009 to show support for local television. The issue is that local TV stations maintain their operations mainly from advertisement revenues. Due to the current economic downturn, several companies have cut back on their advertisement budgets which in turn created financial hardship for many local television stations. According to the CTV campaign, "current regulations in Canada allow cable and satellite companies to take CTV and 'A' programming without compensation. These companies then charge you, the consumer, for the programming they take for free. Most TV subscribers in Canada hold the false belief that part of their basic monthly bills goes to their local TV stations. This isn't true. Television service providers, including cable and satellite companies, are reaping huge profits at the direct expense of local Canadian TV stations that are going out of business. As a consumer, you are at risk of losing local programming options on the dial".

CTV is trying to convince CRTC that local TV stations, like CTV and 'A', should receive compensation from cable and satellite companies that carry their local programming. To protect consumers, they are calling for a review of how cable and satellite companies bundle and bill consumers for the TV channels. CTV is campaigning to receive a fee of 50 cents per subscriber per month from satellite and cable companies, and is asking the CRTC to impose a "fee-for-carriage." CTV is hoping that a strong public support will get the attention of CRTC and influence their decision in favour of local stations. Cable and satellite companies oppose the campaign and have indicated that such fees would be passed on to the consumers. CRTC should view these threats in the light of existing financial revenues. While local stations are struggling to survive, cable companies are making huge profits. For example, according to report (April 2009) in the Marketing Magazine, Cable company revenues were $8.24 billion in 2008, a 16.1% increase from $7.10 billion the previous year. Operating profits before taxes and interest last year were $2.1 billion, up from $1.5 billion in 2007, while the number of basic cable service subscribers increased by 2.9% to 7.9 million. While expenditures were up 7.8%, cable companies enjoyed an increased profit margin of 25.3% in 2008, up from 21.2% in 2007. Digital satellite and multipoint distribution system companies saw a huge jump in operating profits to $81.4 million, from just $17.1 million in 2007—a 376% increase. It was the second consecutive year of profit growth for these companies.

As a cable TV customer I strongly feel that it is time to review how cable and satellite companies bundle and bill customers for the TV channels. The existing bundles include several channels that contain poor programs that we viewers should not have to pay for. There should be options concerning which channels are to be included in the bundle. For example, I would not choose the channels which broadcast extreme religious materials, sexually implicit scenes, constant sports coverage, just to name a few. But, I would likely place channels with local programming on the top of the priority list along with Treehouse TV (my grandchildren watch this station every day and even I became the fan of Dora and Bob the Builder). Consequently, I would support any rulings by the CRTC that would take some of my cable TV charges to support local television.

Where is the Logic?

On Sunday April 5th 2009 I watched the Television program called 60 Minutes on CBS. Cancer patients in the U.S. have been denied treatment because of budget cuts due to the down turn of the economy.

During the economic crisis, public hospitals in the U.S. are needed more than ever. For those without insurance, the county hospital can be their last resort. Yet, recently 12,000 letters went out across Las Vegas telling cancer patients that the only public hospital in the state was closing its outpatient clinic for chemotherapy. One of the cancer patients, Helen Sharp, got such a letter and referred to it as a death sentence. Ms. Sharp, 63, has been fighting lymphoma since July. She's not working because of her illness and has no insurance. Last year, she received charity care at the county hospital, University Medical Center. She was interviewed on 60 Minutes and said in an emotional interview: I don't want to die. I shouldn't have to die. This is a county hospital. This is for people that, like me, many people have lost their insurance, have not any other resources. I mean I was a responsible person. I bought my house. I put money away. I raised my two children. And now I have nothing. You know my house isn't worth anything. I have no money. And I said 'What do I do, but what do all these other people do after me? And they said we don't know".

The story of Ms. Sharp caught my attention particularly because I am also a cancer patient. But I am fortunate to be living in Canada under a universal health care system, and my radiation treatment continued even when my income dropped more than 50% and now I am a cancer survivor. On the other hand, my son, daughter in law, grandson and granddaughter live in the states (they are U.S. citizens) and they have to rely on insurance. While they work, they can pay for the insurance, so they are covered. But what if? ... as a father I am scared for them.

Since the world is going through some tough economic crisis, it is time to reflect on social and economic infrastructures and make the world a better place to live for our children and grandchildren. In particular, we need to make improvements to status quo in the following areas:

1. Millions of dollars are being spent on wars. For example, the war in Iraq was based on false information and has cost to date 4,266 members of the U.S. military and over US$600 billion. Some of that money would be better spent on the needy,

including health care and the essentials of every day living.

2. CEO's of some companies have taken millions of dollars in "bonuses" even while they were laying-off staff and running the company in a way that investors lost most of their savings and former employees ended up with reduced or no pensions at all.

3. Some banks have been tough on individuals who could not service their loan due to loss of work while millions were risked in terms of loans or bad investments to large companies.

4. Some credit card companies increased their service charges up to 24% when individuals were going through difficult times due to job losses and illnesses such as cancer.

It is time for our political leaders to implement safety measures that such abuses on ordinary citizens are curtailed or hopefully eliminated.

English as a Second Language

English can be challenging for foreigners, i.e., for those whose mother-tongue is a different language. I was 18 years old when I ended up in Halifax, Yorkshire and for 9 months I was learning this new language which was so different from the one called the "Queen's English"... you know the one we used to hear when listening to BBC. Then, my next destination was Edinburgh University where most of the professors had a Scottish accent. In those days, the dictionary was my constant companion.

After graduating, I joined the British Colonial Service, which had a language of its one. We were instructed to sign letters as: "I am, Sir, Your Obedient Servant"

Over the years, the culture changed to signing letters as: "Yours faithfully" even though to people you never met..."Yours sincerely" even though to people you didn't trust..."Cheers" even though when you were not having a drink..."Regards" this one I liked and I am still using it.

I was a bit confused when I was learning to drive an automobile. The instructor told me: "Go ahead, back up"...I asked, "which one you want me to do?" I was then asked to park the car on the driveway after driving it on the parkway.

My next challenge was to learn the language used in restaurants. I grew up in Hungary where pork was the popular choice for meat. So in an English restaurant, I was looking forward to having a hamburger. Was I ever surprised when I got beef in a bun! I even got a strange look from the waitress when I asked: "where is the ham?"

I have been especially amused with how children learn to master the English language. About 12 years ago, one of our grandchildren, Marcus, came to visit us. He was proud to tell me that he got a dog for his birthday. I asked him: 'What do you call your dog?" he said "Barky" I thought that was appropriate for a poppy. Then Marcus proceeded to say: "Papa, my dog was broken, but it's OK now because my Dad got him fixed".

Some interesting uses of the English language occur in Church Bulletins where the writers are not necessarily foreigners. For example:

"The Fasting & Prayer Conference includes meals".

"The sermon this morning: Jesus Walks on Water. The sermon tonight: Searching for Jesus".

"Ladies, don't forget the rummage sale. It's a chance to get rid of those things not worth keeping around the house. Bring your husbands"

"Don't let worry kill you off - let the Church help".

"Miss Charlene Mason sang 'I will not pass this way again,' giving obvious pleasure to the congregation".

"At the evening service tonight, the sermon topic will be 'What Is Hell?' Come early and listen to our choir practice".

"This evening at 7 PM there will be a hymn singing in the park across from the Church. Bring a blanket and come prepared to sin".

"Low Self Esteem Support Group will meet Thursday at 7 PM. Please use the back door".

"Weight Watchers will meet at 7 PM at the First Presbyterian Church. Please use large double door at the side entrance".

"The Associate Minister unveiled the church's new tithing campaign slogan last Sunday: 'I Upped My Pledge - Up Yours'."

Promotional slogans can also confuse people who are trying to learn the language. Recently I saw this sign on a restaurant attached to a gas station: "Kids with gas eat free".

I found oxymoron expressions to be the most challenging to understand when I was learning

English. Expressions such as: "jumbo shrimp", "death benefits", and "open secret" can be confusing when you are trying to master the language.

Still, English is a delightful language. Even with misuses, accents, double meanings and other challenges, we manage to understand each other